VGM Opportunities Series

OPPORTUNITIES IN
INTERNATIONAL
BUSINESS CAREERS

Jeffrey S. Arpan

Foreword by
Raymond Oneidas
Vice-President of Human Resources and Organization Development
Schering-Plough Corporation,
International Division

VGM Career Horizons
a division of *NTC Publishing Group*
Lincolnwood, Illinois USA

Cover Photo Credits:
Clockwise from upper left: Leo Burnett (Mr. Yoshiki Ejima);
Colgate-Palmolive; NCR Corporation; Monterey Institute of International
Studies.

Library of Congress Cataloging-in-Publication-Data

Arpan, Jeffrey S.
   Opportunities in international business careers / Jeffrey S.
Arpan.
     p. cm. — (VGM opportunities series)
   Includes bibliographical references.
   ISBN 0-8442-4423-6(hard). — ISBN 0-8442-4424-4 (soft)
    1. International business enterprises—Vocational guidance.
I. Title. II. Series.
HD2755.5.A76   1995
331.7′02—dc20   94-20726
                                                  CIP

Published by VGM Career Horizons, a division of NTC Publishing Group
4255 West Touhy Avenue
Lincolnwood (Chicago), Illinois 60646-1975, U.S.A.

4 5 6 7 8 9 0 VP 9 8 7 6 5 4 3 2 1

CONTENTS

ABOUT THE AUTHOR

Jeffrey Arpan is the James F. Kane Professor of International Business and Director of the International Business Program area at the University of South Carolina. At age 24, he was the youngest person to receive a doctoral degree in international business from Indiana University, and his doctoral dissertation was selected by the Academy of International Business as the best international business dissertation completed in 1971. Other honors he has received include being selected in 1976 as one of the "Outstanding Young Men in America," receiving an award from the American Library Association for being the author of one of the best new reference books published in 1979, and being admitted to Phi Beta Kappa and several other academic honoraries.

From 1971 to 1980, he was a member of the international business faculty at Georgia State University in Atlanta and thereafter joined the international business faculty at the University of South Carolina, becoming director in 1985. His primary teaching interests are international management and strategy, comparative management/cross-cultural communication, and global competitive analysis.

His primary research interests include foreign investments in the United States, the international competitiveness of U.S. industries, business in the Pacific Basin, and international business education. Because of his expertise in these areas, he has frequently been invited to testify before congressional committees and to appear on television news programs investigating these topics. He is also active in executive development programs at USC and for companies such as IBM, Westinghouse, and General Electric.

His more than two decades of teaching, research, and consulting in international business, combined with his world travels and frequent interaction with government officials and international business practitioners and academics, provide him with unique insights about international business and careers in this increasingly important field.

FOREWORD

In a world that seems to be getting smaller every year by virtue of worldwide and 24-hour coverage of global political, sports, and business events, it is easy to be attracted to careers in the international arena. The idea of traveling and living abroad, meeting interesting people, learning new languages, and experiencing new cultures can be very appealing to many people, even if such careers may pose interesting personal challenges for them in the future. In this book, Dr. Arpan captures the essence of what everyone should know and consider before embarking on an international career. By providing a balanced perspective of the pluses and minuses of such careers, Dr. Arpan puts the reader squarely in the driver's seat to decide if international work is right for him or her.

Having worked with many executives, managers, and professionals in the international arena over the past 15 years, it is apparent to me that international work requires a special commitment, very specific skills and abilities, and a strong interest in world events.

Dr. Arpan aptly describes what rewards, as well as risks, exist for those who choose to go international. His profile of those who are best suited for this type of work should not be taken lightly. While exciting, diversified, challenging, and fulfilling on the one hand, the world of international is equally complex, unpredictable, and frustrating on the flip side. Despite these cautions, there are more reasons than ever to consider an international career in business or academia. Today, established, as well as emerging, multinational corporations need people who understand how business functions around the world—not just what works in New York, Chicago, or Los Angeles. Likewise, leading academic institutions recognize that they must have a faculty that is equipped and experienced to provide their students with a broader knowledge and understanding of world business events and geopolitics. Issues related to NAFTA, the EEC, and Japan-U.S. trade relations are as important as domestic economic or marketing trends during this growing era of globalization and transnationalism.

Having or developing an interest in an international career is only the beginning—making it a reality is what really counts. In this regard, Dr. Arpan provides some extremely valuable insights, ranging from the educational track one has to follow early on to getting a job and managing an international career. If you are serious about pursuing either a business or academic career in international, you should carefully read the last two chapters of the book since they provide very useful and practical ideas and "how-to's" on getting started as well as progressing in this arena.

The bottom line is that there are no shortcuts to an international career, but the rewards can be very fulfilling. Having clear career goals, working hard to prepare oneself both academically and on the job, and being persistent as well as patient are the basic ingredients for future success in an arena that offers never-ending challenge, diversity, and change.

> Raymond Oneidas
> Vice-President of Human Resources
> and Organization Development
> Schering-Plough Corporation,
> International Division

PREFACE

International business is all around us. It's the products we buy: imports—products made in this country by foreign-owned companies and parts of products manufactured abroad that become ultimately assembled in this country. It's the places where we work, shop, bank, and vacation that are owned by foreign investors. It's Americans traveling abroad, and foreigners traveling in the United States. It affects the amount of money available for investment, lending, and borrowing and the terms under which they are done, domestically and internationally. It affects the availability, variety, quality, and prices of most products and services offered domestically and internationally. And directly and indirectly, it affects the jobs, personal incomes, and standards of living of most people in this country and throughout the world.

More than ever before, international business increasingly affects all of us—favorably, unfavorably, and occasionally both. As a result, it is increasingly important for everyone to understand how it affects their lives and livelihood. In addition, there are increasing numbers of careers related to international business in business, government, and education, but there continues to be a shortage of people suitably trained for these careers.

The major purpose of this book is to provide information about careers in international business, especially those in business (practitioner careers) and teaching (academic careers). To do this, specific chapters cover such topics as what kinds of jobs exist; where they are located; what challenges, rewards, and risks they bring; and how to prepare for and obtain jobs in international business. In addition, there are sections about the evolution and future of international business and the reasons international business occurs at all.

This book is intended for readers who know little or nothing about international business and the many types of careers that are related to it. It should be equally appropriate for readers who are simply curious and those who are seriously considering a career in international business. However, because the potential audience is so large and diverse and because international business is so complicated, multifaceted, and dynamic, many simplifications and generalizations had to be made in writing this book. In addition, not every type of career in international business is listed or discussed. For all these reasons, this book is more of an abridged overview than a definitive encyclopedia. I offer my apologies at the outset to those whose jobs in international business I have not mentioned at all or have mentioned in too summary a fashion as well as to other professionals in international business who can correctly point out numerous exceptions to my observations, analysis, and conclusions.

In preparing this book, I wish to acknowledge publicly and gratefully several people who contributed to it in various ways. To Sarah Kennedy, the VGM Career Horizons editor who shepherded the revision process. To Annette Selden, who once again masterfully copyedited the final manuscript and in the process made me appear more literate and intelligible than I actually am. To Raymond Oneidas of Schering Plough International, who so willingly and thoughtfully provided the foreword to this book and who has been an international mentor to so many individuals, including me. To the many other international business practitioners and educators who have taught me about international business and whose collective wisdom is very much a part of this book. And finally, to my wife Luz, my daughters Laura, Amy, and Piper, and my son Alejandro who are constant marvels and inspirations to me and to whom this book is dedicated.

CHAPTER 1

INTERNATIONAL BUSINESS: AN IMPORTANT FIELD

In a very short time, there have been momentous changes in the world's political economy. What we knew as the Soviet Union, Yugoslavia, and Czechoslovakia no longer exist. The Warsaw Pact has been dissolved. Canada and the United States first enacted a trade agreement, which was subsequently extended to include Mexico, creating the North American Free Trade Agreement (NAFTA). The former European Community, now renamed the European Union, moved still closer to its goals of full economic and political integration, and Brazil, Argentina, Paraguay, and Uruguay established their own new regional economic bloc, MERCOSUR. Democracies and market-oriented economies were established in many countries that had not had them in decades, if ever, in their history. There were are least a dozen new countries established in the world. New types of national leaders emerged around the world as well as new types of challenges and regional and world issues such as the global AIDS epidemic, global warming, and other ecological problems and concerns. The size and world rank of Japanese corporations reached a historic high while that of U.S. corporations, for the most part, declined. China became one of the ten biggest economies in the world and the fastest-growing economy among the world's major economic powers. And world trade and investment continued to expand and diversify.

In essence, the global political economy has expanded and become even more dynamic than ever before. For virtually all countries, international business accounts for an increasingly large percentage of their gross domestic product. For virtually all companies, international business developments have an increasing impact on their growth or survival. As a result, the demand continues to increase for academicians and business personnel who understand how the global economy works and how to work effectively in the global economy. So while there were many opportunities for international business careers five years ago, today there are greater opportunities. Tomorrow, there will be even greater opportunities.

While changes and new trends in the world affect international business, the activity of international business is centuries old. And not only is international business affected by changes, it has made its own contribution to cultural, political, and economic change throughout history. Nearly a thousand years B.C., ancient Phoenician sailors spread the products and ideas of the Near East, including an early alphabet, as far as Britain and southern Africa. In the eleventh century, the expansion of trade and the resulting growth in the Western European economy led to the development of insurance, modern banking practices, and the reappearance of towns that had all but disappeared; this medieval international business also made possible the great cultural achievements of the Renaissance.

Modern international business has become so widespread and pervasive that it affects virtually everyone, everywhere. Every day of the year, some kind of international business takes place in the United States and throughout the world. If you type your research paper on a computer, drive a car, watch television, eat fruit, or play Nintendo, you probably have experienced the results of international business. Yet despite its importance, there remain many misconceptions about what international business is. And because of these misconceptions, most people do not understand how important it is, what opportunities it offers, or how their lives are affected by it.

BROADENING PERCEPTIONS

People generally have only a vague idea of what international business actually is. To most people, international business involves only the world's largest corporations who build manufacturing facilities in other countries and sell products internationally. This is a very limited perception of who and what international business involves.

In broadest terms, international business is any business activity that occurs between people or organizations from different countries. In actual practice, there are many different kinds of international business carried on between different kinds of people and companies. For example, Americans traveling to a foreign country or foreigners traveling to the United States is international business. Americans purchasing a foreign-made product or foreigners purchasing a product made by an American company is international business. Shopping at a store in the United States owned by a foreign company or working in the United States for a company owned by a foreign firm is international business. Investing in a mutual fund that includes stock of foreign companies is also international business. These are only a few examples of different kinds of international business. However, in this book emphasis is placed on the two major kinds of international business in terms of volume, value, and importance. These two kinds are international trade and international investment.

INTERNATIONAL TRADE

When a person or company in one country sells a product to someone or a company in another country, the transaction is called an export. If a person or company buys a product from someone or a company in another country, the transaction is called an import. Together, imports and exports comprise what is referred to as international trade.

In addition to products, services of various types can also be imported or exported. For example, if a U.S. citizen buys an airline ticket to Europe from a French airline company, the United States considers this a service import, and France considers it a service export. This example illustrates the dual nature of all international business transactions. An import viewed from one country's perspective is an export viewed from the other country's perspective.

Thousands of different products and services are exported and imported each year by the United States and other countries. One major category is raw materials, such as coal, tin, copper, rubber, and oil. Another major category is agricultural products, such as wheat, corn, soybeans, and cotton. A third major category is semifinished goods used in the production of other goods, such as computer chips, chemicals, seats and engines for automobiles, and fabrics for clothes. A fourth major category is finished products, such as transportation vehicles, computers, video recorders, televisions, shoes, and foods and beverages. The final major category is services, such as transportation services, consulting services, and financial services.

INTERNATIONAL INVESTMENT

If a company builds a manufacturing facility in another country, it is making a kind of international investment called a direct investment. Other kinds of direct investments include establishing in another country a sales office, warehousing facility, branch office, or some other kind of representative office. Another form of direct investment is buying land, commercial property (such as an office building or shopping center), or a farm in another country. Direct investments also include joint ventures, collaborative investments made with another company.

If a company or person buys only a few shares of a foreign company's stock or buys some government bonds of a foreign country, it is making a kind of international investment called an indirect or portfolio investment. Other forms of capital flows include making a loan to a person or company in another country or borrowing money from a person or company in another country.

The basic difference between direct and indirect investments is the intention of the investor. If the intent is to control the activities of the investment, it is a direct investment. If the intent is not to control, it is an indirect investment.

As is the case with international trade, international investment occurs in two directions. American companies such as IBM and General Motors build manufacturing facilities overseas, and foreign companies such as Toyota and Michelin build manufacturing facilities in the United States. American banks such as Chase Manhattan and Bank of America loan money to foreign companies and governments, and foreign banks such as Barclays and the Bank of Tokyo loan money to American companies and the U.S. government.

INTERNATIONAL TRADE: A NECESSITY

The Need to Import

There are many reasons international trade takes place. One main reason is that people in one country need to have something that is not available in their own country but is available in another country. For example, virtually all countries need oil, but not all countries have supplies of oil. Or most countries need gold, but only a few have gold deposits. In other situations, a country may have some quantities of something it needs but not a sufficient quantity to satisfy the demand for the product. For example, it produces food but not in sufficient quantities to feed its population. Or there is some money available for investing or borrowing but not enough to fulfill the domestic demand. In these situations, international business (in this case, importing goods or money) occurs because of an unfulfilled need.

In other cases, people may have unfulfilled wants or preferences for products or services that do not exist in their country. Or they do not exist in the quantity, quality, or variety desired. For example, while people really do not need VCRs, they may want them anyway. Or they might not be able to buy a high-quality wine in their own country, even though such wines are readily available in another country. In these situations, international business may and often does occur, even though it is not based on a real economic need.

The Need to Export

Thus, the primary reason that international business takes place is because people in one country want or need something that does not exist at all in their country or does not exist in sufficient quantity, quality, or variety in their country. However, in order to get (import) products or services from another country, you normally have to pay the foreign supplier (unless the supplier is willing to donate the product or service). And in most cases you have to pay in the currency of the supplier's country. In other words, foreign suppliers usually want to be paid in the kind of money they can use in their own countries. For example, French suppliers prefer to be paid in francs, Japanese suppliers in yen, and Brazilian suppliers in cruzados, Therefore, a person, company, or country that wants to import something must be able to obtain foreign currencies to pay for what it wants to import. And the primary way foreign currencies can be obtained is by selling (exporting) a product or service to other countries. Thus, the need or desire to import results in the need to export.

For example, if the United States wants to buy something from Japan that will require payment in Japanese yen, the United States will need to sell something to Japan that it wants. In this manner, the United States gets yen from the Japanese purchasers of its products and can then use these yen to pay for the products it buys from Japan. Or stated in another way, the Japanese earn dollars to pay for what they import from the United States by selling something to the United States.

All international trade is not driven by a need to import, however. There are many instances when exports occur that are not related to import considerations. For example, a domestic company may see that the domestic demand for its products is declining. Or the company may observe that the domestic demand for its products is not growing as rapidly as the demand for its products in other countries. In either situation, a company desiring to increase its total sales and profits (or prevent greater decline in them) may decide on its own to export its products. In reality, much international trade is driven by individual companies' desires to export rather than import. However, a company's ability to export depends on its having the kind of product or service that is in demand in other countries. It also depends on the ability of foreign customers to pay for the product or services being offered. For example, in order for a U.S. company to export to Japan, the Japanese customer (importer) must be able to have sufficient dollars to pay the

U.S. exporter, or the U.S. exporter must be willing to accept payment in yen. The latter case might occur if the U.S. firm needs to import something from Japan (and therefore can use the yen it receives), or if it can sell the yen it receives to some other company who needs yen.

The Two-Way Nature of International Trade

All of the U.S.-Japan examples just described illustrate the necessary two-way nature of all international business transactions viewed from a company's or country's perspective. In the aggregate, in order to import something a country must be able to export something of comparable value. Both ideally and in theory, the value of a country's exports should equal the value of what it imports. In other words, its international trade (imports and exports) should be perfectly balanced.

In reality, however, seldom is a country able to perfectly balance its international trade at every point in time. The more usual case is that a country either imports more than it exports or exports more than it imports. If it imports more than it exports, it has an international trade deficit. If it exports more than it imports, it has an international trade surplus. For example, the United States currently has a trade deficit with Japan, while Japan has a trade surplus with the United States. The reason is that Americans are buying more Japanese products than Japanese are buying American products.

In addition, the United States has a trade deficit with the world as a whole even though it has trade surpluses with several countries. The basic reason the United States has a trade deficit with the world as a whole is the same reason the United States has a trade deficit with Japan: the United States is importing more products and services than it is exporting.

INTERNATIONAL CAPITAL FLOWS

International trade deficits and surpluses give rise to another form of international business activity: international capital flows. If a country has a trade deficit, it must transfer some of its wealth (capital) to the countries with whom it has trade deficits. Stated another way, if it cannot export enough to a country to earn the money to pay for what it is importing from that country, it will have to use its own money to pay for the imports. Thus, the current trade deficit of the United States results in some of the accumulated wealth of the United States being transferred to other countries. In short, the United States is losing some of its wealth to other countries. This is one form of an international capital flow.

On the other hand, Japan's huge trade surpluses allow it to loan some of its money to other countries or to invest some of it in other countries where there are higher returns available than in Japan. Thus, international lending and investing are two other kinds of international capital flows that result from funds generated by international trade. However, they also can and do occur for other reasons.

In some cases, the financial returns on an investment are higher in other countries than they are domestically. Smart investors will want to earn as high a return as possible on their investments. Therefore, if they are permitted to do so, they will invest their funds in those countries where their financial returns will be highest (taking into account different degrees of financial risk). For example, if the profitability from investing in a U.S. government treasury bond is higher than from investing in a Mexican government treasury bond, Mexican investors will prefer to invest in U.S. treasury bonds and bring their money into the United States. Similarly, if the risk of investing money in one country is higher than investing it in another country, investment capital may flow from the more risky country to the less risky country (taking into account the different financial returns available). These two examples illustrate international capital flows that are driven primarily by a desire to earn a higher financial return or a less risky return. However, a large percentage of international capital flows occur primarily to support (finance) various types of other international business activities.

Consider the case of a U.S. manufacturer that sees a need to manufacture its product in a foreign country. This need may result from greater business opportunities outside the United States or from its inability to export to a foreign market because of that foreign country's trade restrictions on imports. It can also result from the company's desire to reduce its risk of operating in only one country or to produce itself some products or components of final products more cheaply abroad than it can domestically. In any of these situations, the company will need funds in order to make the investment abroad, and it will need these funds in the foreign country. If it uses funds from the United States, what results is an international capital outflow from the United States called a direct international investment. If it borrows or otherwise raises the needed funds for the investment in the foreign country, it is still a direct investment, but the actual capital outflow from the United States is delayed until the foreign loan's interest or principal is repaid or dividends are paid to the foreign stockholders. The same kinds of effects occur (only in reverse) when a foreign manufacturer builds a facility in the United States.

Finally, a few comments about the international operations of financial institutions are needed in order to complete the big picture of international business activities. To earn the highest and safest returns for their own funds and the funds others place at their disposal, financial institutions themselves make international investments. However, they also borrow or otherwise raise money abroad in order to increase the money they can have available to loan to their customers for domestic or international use. In addition, even if they do not obtain or invest money abroad, they often loan money to domestic or foreign firms to finance international trade and investments. These latter types of activities are typically referred to as international financial services and are driven by the need to better service the clients (customers) of the financial institutions.

A PROFOUND IMPACT ON SOCIETY

More than ever before, international business is influencing the lives of virtually every person and organization in the world. Because of international trade, people in all countries have a greater variety of goods and services to consume. International trade also results in lower prices and a greater range of quality. International investments affect the supply of available funds to be lent or borrowed in any country and the price (interest rate) of lending and borrowing. International trade and investment flows also affect government deficits and the international purchasing power of all countries' currencies. In addition, millions of jobs are related directly or indirectly to international trade and international investment.

It is reasonable to assume that international business will have an increasingly important impact on society in the future. There will be both positive and negative impacts on various segments of society and on society as a whole. Stated another way, some groups will benefit more than others from international business, and some groups, such as employees who lose their jobs as a result of international competition, will actually be hurt by international business. For any society, the task ahead will be to maximize the societal gains (benefits) from international business and minimize the losses. This same task applies to individuals.

In addition, because international business is influenced directly and indirectly by government policies, all citizens need to participate intelligently in government policy deliberations and actions concerning international business, even if they themselves are not working in international business. Every year, government officials deliberate and enact legislation that affects international trade and investment flows. Therefore, it is important that all government officials and those who elect them have a thorough and realistic understanding of how international business affects their society and the larger world. Thus, it is everyone's economic, political, and societal obligation to become better informed about, and more capable of dealing effectively with, international business. If not, there will be many unintentional consequences of the actions we take or do not take, both individually and collectively.

In sum, hardly a day will go by without virtually everyone being affected by international business, no matter where they live or what they do for a living. Therefore, wise individuals will equip themselves with the skills and attitudes necessary for success in an international-ized society.

A PRACTITIONER CAREER IN BUSINESS

Before deciding whether a career in international business is right for you, you must first decide whether a career in business is right for you. There are literally hundreds of different jobs in business, each involving different activities, skills, and attitudes. But in essence, all businesses have a common goal: to provide a product or service to a customer. And in most cases, businesses seek to do so at a profit, an exception being not-for-profit businesses such as public hospitals and public transportation.

The specific activities businesses perform can be grouped broadly into eight categories: accounting, finance, purchasing, logistics, produc-tion, marketing, personnel, and management. In addition to these basic activities common to all businesses, most firms also conduct research and service activities. And in most large businesses, a person tends to specialize and work in only one of these areas of activity. In smaller firms, a person may often be involved in more than one of these activities.

Accounting

Accounting involves keeping records of financial activities and preparing related reports for use inside and outside the firm. Therefore, accountants collect, prepare, analyze, store, and distribute information to others who need to know how well the firm is doing. Without such information nobody would know how much a product costs, how much money is needed to operate the business, how much profit was made, what supplies need to be ordered, how much salaries can be increased, and much more.

Within the field of accounting, there are several different types of accountants, and accounting activities. These different types are ex-plained in greater detail in chapter 5.

Finance

Finance involves obtaining money for a business to get started and to operate and finding the best ways to distribute or invest the money resulting from operations. It also involves making sure that money is not being wasted or used ineffectively and that there is sufficient money available for operations currently and in the future. In addition to reporting to management, finance people interact with those who have loaned money to, or invested money in, the company as well as with those who owe the company money. There is a close working relationship between people working in finance and accounting as a result.

Purchasing/Procurement

To provide a product or service, firms must obtain the necessary supplies and materials from other companies or other divisions of their own companies. This activity is called purchasing or procurement. Purchasers must learn where the necessary supplies can be obtained and then negotiate for their acquisition according to factors such as price, quality, special features, delivery schedules, and terms of payment. In deciding what to purchase, purchasers typically rely on information provided by their firm's production managers.

Logistics

Logistics focuses on the physical movement (transportation) of goods into and out of a firm. For a manufacturing firm, inbound logistics refers to selecting the method of delivery to be used for each item purchased from another company or affiliate. Outbound logistics does the same for goods sold by the company to other companies or affiliates. In the process of selecting the method of transportation to be used in either direction, logistics takes into account the speed, dependability, cost, and quality of the transportation method and transporting company as well as the type of services provided by the carrier. In some cases, it also involves complying with certain laws, regulations and business/social customs that may dictate how goods must be transported. In today's increasingly competitive world, logistics has increased in importance because of the real cost savings and greater customer satisfaction that it can generate.

Production

Production involves the conversion of supplies and materials into a finished product. From a product design, production managers must determine how to manufacture the product as effectively and efficiently as possible while still meeting the needs of the final customer. These decisions include where to manufacture the product, what materials are needed, what production process to use, what the production schedule should be, and quality considerations. Much of the information they need to make these decisions is obtained from the marketing personnel who must ultimately sell the product to the customers.

Marketing

Marketing involves finding out what people want to buy, designing these products and services, and then promoting and selling them to the ultimate customers. Considerable research must be done to conduct all of these activities properly. In addition, much time and effort must be expended to convince potential customers that the firm's product or service best fits the potential customers' specific needs and preferences. Marketing also involves obtaining and analyzing feedback from existing customers about their satisfaction with the product or service supplied by the firm. This process identifies ways in which the products or services may need to be changed in the future.

Personnel/Human Resources

The area of personnel (now more typically called human resources) is concerned with the employee-related aspects of the firm. Examples include hiring and firing, promotions, wages and benefits, working conditions, employee training, and the many facets of management-employee relations. In its broadest sense, the function of employee relations is to attract, train, and keep the best personnel needed for successful operation of the business.

Management

The basic job of management is to keep every aspect of the business running smoothly and as effectively and efficiently as possible. While management activities exist in all of the other areas discussed, it is the responsibility of top management to plan, coordinate, and control the activities of all of the other areas. Without proper planning, coordination, and control, the business will not operate as successfully as it could and, in the worst case, may cease to operate entirely. Therefore, management positions are of the utmost importance to the firm and require people with superior technical expertise and leadership abilities.

Research and Service

Not all firms are involved in research and service activities; often many rely on other firms to conduct these activities for them. However, most firms do conduct these activities themselves in order to be more competitive.

In practice, *research* involves a wide range of activities including basic and applied research. An example of basic research is the study of the different conductivity of various metals. An example of applied research is analyzing how the conductivity of a particular metal can be utilized in particular products to improve their performance and marketability. The objective of research is to develop better products or better production processes.

Service refers to activities performed by the firm for its customers to help them better utilize the firm's product. It also includes keeping products in proper working condition or replacing defective ones. While service functions are often technical, they are also an effective marketing tool.

Chapter 5 of this book contains information about the international dimensions of each of these basic activities of business. Other chapters include information about working conditions and rewards in international business, where most international business jobs are located, and how you can prepare yourself for a career in international business as a practitioner or teacher.

Generally, it is safe to say that the activities are essentially the same in both domestic and international business. However, the international dimensions are more complicated and challenging and therefore require more specialized skills and techniques and a more flexible outlook and attitude.

AN ACADEMIC CAREER IN BUSINESS

There are many differences between a practitioner career and an academic career in business or any other field. In the most general sense, an academic career offers a very different life-style—one that is more intellectually stimulating and challenging, more self-directed, slower paced, and, in many instances, more secure from an employment perspective. On the negative side, academics generally are paid less and receive less attractive benefit packages than practitioners. As a result of these differences, some people are more suited and attracted to an academic career and some to a practitioner career. Careers in international business are no exception.

As discussed earlier in this chapter, there is an increasing need for skilled practitioners in international business. As a result, there is also an increasing need for people who can properly prepare and train people for business careers in an international setting. Examples include teachers of foreign languages and cultures; international politics, economics, and geography; and, of course, the international aspects of business. These kinds of teachers are needed at all levels of the formal education system, from primary schools through universities. They are also needed in a wide range of continuing education programs for people already employed in business or government service. In fact, it can be argued that they are needed everywhere to help people understand how international business influences their lives. In other words, a better internationally informed and trained work force (and general population) will result in a better world for everyone.

The working conditions, financial and psychological rewards, and the preparation required for an academic career in the international business field are not always the same as those related to a career as an international business practitioner. Therefore, most of the subsequent chapters of this book begin with a practitioner focus but conclude with a separate section focusing on academic careers in international business.

CHAPTER 2

THE EVOLUTION OF INTERNATIONAL BUSINESS

PAST TRENDS IN INTERNATIONAL BUSINESS

In the past, international business was conducted for essentially the same reason that it is today and will be in the future: profit. However, the types of international business activities have changed, as have the types of business organizations conducting international business. In addition, the magnitude and geographic scope of international business have increased considerably. Understanding how international business evolved and how it has changed will help you understand where it is headed in the future.

A HISTORICAL OVERVIEW

The first written records of international business activity date back to the very beginning of written history (roughly 3,000 B.C.). However, there is some evidence of a nonwritten nature that suggests international business occurred even earlier. Strictly speaking, it was not really international business, because there were not any nations until much later. But for practical purposes, trade was taking place among people of different cultures, primarily involving luxury products.

The Greeks and Romans

Trading nonluxury goods of a comparatively inexpensive and mass-produced variety began in earnest primarily with the Greeks around the fifth century B.C.. Also at this time, international trading became a full-time occupation for many of the people who previously had traded on a part-time basis. Several centuries later, it was the Romans who moved to the forefront of trading. During the time of the Roman Empire, there was considerable freedom of movement of people, goods, and money throughout a vast geographical area encompassing Europe and the Middle East. Trade was also facilitated by a common monetary unit (the dinarius) used throughout most of the Roman Empire. Because of the common currency, all trade did not have to be conducted on a swap basis. For example, if you wanted to sell clothes, you no longer had to receive payment in the form of some other product; instead, you could receive payment in dinars almost anywhere. But like today, only those products that offered the highest profit potential were likely to be traded internationally.

The Middle Ages

During the Middle Ages, several trends began that were to continue to influence international business today. One was the importance to a country or city of having a strategic location in terms of trade routes. After the Fall of Rome, the focal point for international trade became the area where most north-south and east-west trade routes converged: Byzantium (now known as Constantinople). Not only did Byzantium become dominant in trading activity but its currency became the dominant currency for trade. It has remained almost a truism in international business that the most important trading nation's currency becomes the most important currency in international business.

Also during this period, the forerunners of financial services, organizations we now refer to as banks and insurance companies, were established. The development and use of credit encouraged and facilitated the expansion of trade, as did the ability to insure shipments. To further promote trade, major trade fairs began to occur, attracting hundreds of buyers and sellers from different regions to a single location. Such trade fairs continue today on an even larger scale. Other major developments that facilitated and changed the nature of international trade occurred in shipping: more accurate maps and navigational instruments, ships with rudders, and much bigger ships. Having a major seaport and ocean-going ships became crucial for success in international business and prompted the emergence of what is now known as Italy as a major center of international trade and finance.

The Mercantile Period

Government regulation of business activity was a hallmark of this period, which began in the sixteenth century. During the seventeenth and eighteenth centuries, however, it reached its high point. Most governments sought to amass as much wealth as they could whenever and wherever possible. They wanted their citizens to be as prosperous as possible. Among other policies, they encouraged exports and discouraged (regulated) imports. They also established foreign colonies to increase the mother country's wealth. Spain, Portugal, England, France, and the Netherlands were all actively colonizing the world during this period, primarily to gain favorable (cheap) access to raw material abundant in the colonies. In a sense, this was the beginning of international investment. In the process, the colonizing countries also found new markets for their exports: the colonies.

The successful mercantile policies and activities of the Western European countries resulted in still another shift in the location of power in international business, this time from the Mediterranean to Western Europe. For the next three centuries, the most important commercial innovations were to take place in Western Europe, and this region would continue to dominate international trade and investment. Among the most notable innovations were new forms of business organizations: the regulated company, the joint-stock company, and the limited liability company.

Finally, toward the end of this period a new country was established that in later centuries would become the richest nation in the world and would dominate international business activity through the twentieth century: the United States of America. In its infancy, the United States relied heavily on loans and investments from other countries to develop

America's industries and infrastructure. Even today, such loans and investments from other countries remain important to the United States. In addition, the early international trade of the United States was significantly determined and conducted by foreign companies. By the beginning of the twentieth century, however, the economy of the United States and its international business activity were propelled largely by its own efforts. And while international business was expanding rapidly throughout the world, the United States was beginning to exert an influence on international business that would continue to increase during most of the rest of the century.

The 1900s to the 1970s

The rapid industrialization of the United States created major opportunities for international trade. Substantial imports of raw materials, intermediate products, and equipment were needed. In turn, the need for imports and the growing industrial output of the United States required and permitted increased exports. In a relatively short period of time (by historical standards), the United States became one of the major trading nations in the world. The efforts of the U.S. business community were so successful that the size of the U.S. trade surplus soon became the largest in the world. In addition, the U.S. dollar became the dominant currency in the world, replacing the English pound. Also during this period, U.S. companies made substantial investments in other countries, either seeking raw materials or building manufacturing plants to service foreign markets.

The two world wars and the depression of the 1930s significantly disrupted international business activities during the first half of the twentieth century. Maintaining or increasing domestic employment became the primary goal of all countries, and numerous types of government restrictions on international trade and investment were enacted during and immediately following these periods. As a result, the expansion of international business was slowed and, in some cases, virtually stopped. However, most governments realized that employment expansion depended on economic expansion and that economic expansion depended on international business expansion. Therefore, international trade and investment restrictions began to be dismantled in most parts of the world. Several major multination trade agreements were implemented under the auspices of the General Agreement on Trade and Tariffs (GATT). The general purpose of these trade agreements was to reduce significantly existing trade barriers with an eye toward eliminating them altogether. The United States played the key role in promoting the success of the GATT agreements.

One other major development that significantly influenced many international business trends was the creation of the European Economic Community (EEC) in the 1950s, now more appropriately referred to as the European Union (EU). The EU was established to promote economic and political integration among its member nations. This goal was to be accomplished by eliminating all trade and investment restrictions between the member nations, by establishing a uniform set of laws governing all EU countries, by coordinating all countries' monetary and fiscal policies, and by establishing an EU-wide parliamentary body. Also in the plan was the goal of establishing a common currency for all the EU countries. From the original six member countries, the EU has expanded to include nine full-member countries and several associate members.

While all of the goals for the EU have not yet been achieved, its formation did result in a surge of economic development within it. International trade and investment among the member countries increased dramatically, as did the EU members' international trade and investment with the rest of the world. The tremendous economic development in the EU also led to a surge of foreign investments into the EU by U.S. firms. The United States quickly became the biggest foreign investor in the EU and its major trading partner.

By the end of the 1960s, the United States had become the dominant economic power in the world and in volume and value terms was the world's biggest international trader and investor. The U.S. dollar reigned supreme in international money markets, and American companies had established production, sales, and service facilities in virtually every country of the world. However, as history teaches us, economic dominance of the world is a transitory phenomenon. It comes and it goes. And in the 1970s and 1980s, new major competitors were to seriously challenge the economic dominance of the United States in world markets and even in the U.S. domestic market.

CURRENT TRENDS

Current trends are considered to be those beginning primarily in the 1970s and continuing through the year 2000. In general terms, international trade and investment have continuously expanded during this period and have reached new heights. This expansion has occurred amidst major changes in the international monetary system and in the values of currencies, changes in governments, and major changes in the prices of raw materials and final products. And most significantly, international business was influenced by substantial changes in international competitiveness. In the sections that follow, each of the major changes that has influenced international business since the 1970s is discussed separately.

Changes in Currency Values

International business takes place in many different currencies. However, most companies involved in international business ultimately want to end up with their own country's currency. To do this they must always deal in their own currency (which is difficult and sometimes impossible to do) or be able to convert the foreign currencies they receive into their own country's currency.

Any time one currency is exchanged for another currency, there must be an exchange rate that tells how much one currency is worth in terms of the other currency. These rates are called foreign exchange rates. As long as exchange rates do not change, there is no uncertainty about the value of money in one currency in relation to another currency. But if foreign exchange rates change, the value of the foreign currency changes in terms of the domestic currency.

In general terms, if a country's currency decreases in relationship to other countries' currencies, the country's exports become cheaper abroad, but importing foreign products costs more. Thus, we would expect the country's exports to increase and its imports to decrease. In addition, as one country's currency declines, it becomes cheaper for foreign firms to invest in the country but more expensive for the domestic firms to invest abroad. Thus, we would expect incoming foreign investments to increase and outgoing foreign investments to decrease. The same effect would occur with international tourism. When a country's currency declines, it becomes cheaper for foreigners to visit the country but more expensive for domestic citizens to travel abroad. Thus, changes in exchange rates influence the amount, direction, costs, and risks of international business activities. And there have been many changes in exchange rates since the 1970s.

After World War II, most countries agreed to establish the value of their currencies based upon a specific amount of gold or U.S. dollars and to maintain this value in a stable manner (within 1 percent initially and 2.5 percent subsequently). The idea was to stabilize exchange rates and thereby encourage international business. However, this system of fixed exchange rates did not work as intended. Many countries were unable to maintain exchange rates at the fixed amount but resisted making any official changes. When they finally had to make a change, it was often a drastic change that contributed to great disruptions in foreign exchange markets and international business activity. Therefore, in 1976, the member countries of the International Monetary System agreed to accept an option of three exchange rate systems to replace the old fixed-rate system. The first option permitted the fixing of an exchange rate (similar to the previously existing system). The second option permitted the pegging of a currency to another currency, such as the U.S. dollar or British pound. The third option permitted a floating system in which a currency's value would be based on global supply and demand. Most of the developed nations selected the third option, while most of the developing countries selected one of the other two options.

The net result of all of these changes has been significant swings in the exchange rates of many countries, but the swings have been more gradual than abrupt in nature. In addition, the foreign exchange values of many countries' currencies have gone up and down several times. For example, during much of the 1970s, the U.S. dollar's exchange value declined against most of the other major currencies, then increased in value during the first half of the 1980s, then declined sharply in the second half of the 1980s. The strong dollar of the early 1980s led to a big increase in U.S. imports and a big decrease in U.S. exports and caused a huge deficit in the U.S. balance of trade. With the more recent decline in the foreign exchange value of the dollar, U.S. exports are increasing, and U.S. imports are decreasing.

The impact on the United States of changes in exchange rates was similar to the impact of these changes on other countries. As foreign countries' exchange rates rose, it was more difficult for them to export and easier for them to import. All countries' international investment and tourism flows were also affected accordingly. In sum, all countries and most companies had to make adjustments in their strategies and activities because of changes in exchange rates.

Changes in Governments

Major changes in governments have almost always influenced international business trends, and many of those that occurred in the 1970s, 1980s, and 1990s were no exception. The election of Margaret Thatcher as prime minister of Britain led to a resurgence of the British economy and a strengthening of the foreign exchange value of the British pound. On the other hand, the election of François Mitterand as the first socialist president of France initially caused an outflow of investment capital from France and a decline in the exchange value of the franc. Changes in the governments of several developing countries reduced or temporarily halted international business activities for a certain period due to new restrictive laws or increased political and economic uncertainties. The change of government in Iran was perhaps the most striking example.

Even just the possibility of a major change in government can temporarily influence international business. The 1987 presidential election in South Korea was such a case. The international business community and the Korean population were uncertain about whether the candidate of the party in power that had been responsible for Korea's recent economic surge would lose to the candidate of the opposition party that had significantly different plans for Korea's future. Similarly, the potential outcome of the Quebec separatist movement in Canada led some companies to shift their activities to other parts of Canada or to other countries. And Britain's return of Hong Kong to the People's Republic of China in 1997 continues to cause uncertainty among the global business community about investments in and trade with Hong Kong.

Yet by far the most dramatic change in governments in the latter half of the twentieth century was the collapse of what was the Soviet Union. From the early years of Peristroika and Glasnost through the outlawing of the Communist party to the ultimate dissolution and fragmentation, changes in Soviet government policies, parties, and leaders caused major changes in international business patterns and relations between the U.S.S.R. and the rest of the world. Furthermore, the collapse of the Soviet Union had an immediate and dramatic negative impact on the international trade levels and patterns of its major trading partners in the Warsaw Pact and ultimately affected its form of government and economic system. In short, it caused not only a big splash but also many subsequent tidal waves throughout the global political economy.

Finally, the current trend throughout most of the world is toward greater government concern about economic development and business regulation, both internally and internationally. The reason is both simple and complex. The simple reason is that international business is having a much greater impact on domestic, economic, social, and political conditions than it has had previously. As a result, governments have had to become increasingly concerned about these impacts and how to control them to their countries' advantage. The complex reason is that it is very difficult to predict accurately the impacts and even more difficult to control them.

By taking a more active role in business activity and the conditions that influence it (both domestically and internationally), governments believe they can better control the impacts that international business has on their countries. Some forms of government involvement are inwardly directed, essentially trying to protect their domestic firms from foreign competition. Other forms are outwardly directed, essentially trying to increase the competitiveness of their domestic firms in international markets. In all forms, however, government involvement alters international business flows and activities and distorts the results that would have occurred without government involvement.

Changes in Prices

Prices are generally determined by supply and demand. But as prices change, they also influence supply and demand. And in international business during the current period, there have been many significant changes in the prices of most goods and services.

In virtually all countries, income has been rising, and, as a result, consumption demand has risen with it. This has been true for both industrial and consumer demand and has resulted in an increase in the amount of goods and services being offered for sale throughout the world. In most cases, however, there has not been a perfect balance between supply and demand in each country. In some countries, demand has exceeded supply. And unless these countries have restricted imports, the excess demand has been filled by imports. In other countries, domestic demand has not risen enough to satisfy the growth needs of the domestic industry. As a result, companies in these countries have sought to increase their exports to other countries.

In general terms, increased international trade and competition have resulted in the lowering of prices of most products. Just a few examples include the prices of clothes, VCRs, computers, and shoes. However, while good for consumers, the lower prices have not always been good for many manufacturers who cannot profitably produce and sell their products at the lower prices. And if it has not been good for some manufacturers, it has not been good for many employees of these firms. Examples of this problem also abound. Import competition has forced many domestic firms to go out of business, close plants, reduce their employment, or to either reduce their employees' wages or keep wages from rising.

Not all prices have consistently declined during the current period, however, and some prices have actually increased either temporarily or consistently. The most notable swings in prices occurred in crude oil. In the early 1970s, the international price of crude oil was typically less than eight dollars a barrel. In 1974, however, the world's major oil-exporting countries quadrupled the price of oil and temporarily stopped exporting oil to many countries, including the United States.

For the next several years, economic expansion was slowed in virtually all oil-importing countries as a result of the decreased availability of oil and oil's higher prices. Concurrently, the economic wealth and development of the oil-exporting countries increased dramatically. This was particularly true in Arab oil-producing countries such as Saudi Arabia, Iraq, and Kuwait. As a result, a great percentage of international business activity shifted to the Middle East. Then several events converged to bring down the price of oil.

First, oil-importing countries reduced their consumption of oil through conservation, shifting to less expensive energy alternatives, such as coal, or slowing down their economic growth. Second, dissension began to occur among the cartel of oil-exporting countries (the Organization of Petroleum Exporting Countries, or OPEC). Some wanted to increase the supply of oil being exported and lower its price while others wanted to continue to restrict exports and keep prices high. Ultimately, the price of oil began to decline and by the 1980s had fallen to $15 dollars a barrel. With the fall in oil prices, economic activity increased again in most countries, and international business activity shifted away from the Middle East.

In sum, international business during the current period caused major changes in prices and also had to adjust to many changes in prices. Such is the nature and competitive challenge of international business.

Changes in International Competitiveness

Perhaps the most significant trend during the current period is the change in international competitiveness. The United States dominated international business activity from the 1950s through the 1970s, despite a general increase in international business activity by many other countries. The United States had the most money to invest and lend, a significant lead (if not monopoly) in most technologies, the widest range of products to sell, and the world's largest companies and most productive labor force. In sum, the United States was in the driver's seat, and everything looked rosy. Then, bit by bit, the U.S. dominance began to erode.

Perhaps the U.S. business community and labor force became too complacent. Perhaps the U.S. consumer became too consumption oriented. Perhaps the entire country became too short-term oriented and

U.S. government policies became too restrictive. Perhaps other countries were more hungry for economic growth and improving their standards of living and were willing to work harder to achieve them. But for any or all of these reasons, there began to emerge significant competition for U.S. firms in both their domestic and foreign markets. The United States was neither the leader in technology in many areas nor the lowest cost producer. The ranking of U.S. companies among the world's largest companies declined, and in several industries, foreign companies became the largest in the world. U.S. trade surpluses turned into huge trade deficits, and the U.S. changed from being the world's biggest creditor nation to its biggest debtor nation.

Western Europe and Canada were not without their own problems. Unemployment was higher in most of these countries than it was in the United States, and they experienced even more severe import competition in some industries than the United States experienced. Many of their firms' rankings among the world's largest companies also declined and, in most cases, even further than those of U.S. companies. Thus, while conditions were worsening in the United States, they became even worse in most of the Western European nations and in Canada. The notable exceptions were Italy and Germany. These two nations improved significantly their international competitiveness, economically surged ahead of the other European nations, and, in some industries, surged ahead of their U.S. competitors.

If the situation in Western Europe and Canada was generally worse than in the United States, Europe and Canada were still doing better than most countries in Latin America and Africa. For the most part, these regions have continued to fall further and further behind the rest of the world. Many of them are so much in debt to other countries that they are unable to repay the debt, and their political and economic instability hinder prospects for future economic development.

If so many of the world's major countries were losing international competitiveness, who was gaining? Several countries in the Asia-Pacific region. The biggest gainer, without question, has been Japan. Japan has emerged as the second biggest and wealthiest industrial power in the world, and Japan's per-capita income now exceeds that of the United States. Japan now has the largest manufacturing trade surplus in the world and has become the world's largest creditor nation. Many Japanese products have become the standard against which all other countries' products are judged in terms of quality and price performance. In addition, Japan leads the world in many forms of applied technology, and many countries are now imitating Japanese production and management techniques.

However, Japan has not been the only big gainer in the Asia-Pacific region. Korea, Taiwan, Hong Kong, and Singapore have also made impressive gains. Often referred to as the four tigers of Asia, these countries have experienced exponential growth in their domestic economies and in their international business activities. All of them have trade surpluses with the rest of the world and are moving aggressively in virtually all world markets. In fact, they are now competing very successfully with Japan and the United States in many industries and world markets.

Not far behind are the economies of Indonesia, Malaysia, and Thailand. All three of them are expected to continue their rapid economic development and emergence into the global economy and become increasingly important players. And finally, the sleeping giant of Asia, China, began to awaken. With over a billion people and double-digit annual average growth rates during most of the 1990s, China became the world's biggest economic "hot spot" and has positioned itself as a true economic power in the world's most economically explosive region. Thus, as has happened so many times in the past, the center of international business activity has been shifting. This time, it is shifting away from the United States and the Western world to Japan, China, and the Asian world of the Pacific Rim.

FUTURE TRENDS

Predicting the future is always a difficult and imprecise task. Many historical trends will not continue, and entirely new but currently unforeseeable trends are likely to occur. Therefore, be cautious about relying too strictly on any forecast of the future, including the forecast described in this section about future trends in international business. The discussion that follows focuses on the future trends for the most important international business activities: international trade and international investment.

International Trade

It seems logical and safe to predict that international trade will continue to increase in both volume and value in the future. Despite some major interruptions in the world's trade growth in the past, international trade has always resumed in an upward direction. In addition, international trade has continued to become increasingly important to virtually all countries. It is likely to continue to be important because of its generally favorable impact on individual nations and the world's standard of living. We can expect that additional products will be traded internationally and that additional countries will become more actively involved in international trade. As multinational firms continue to expand their activities throughout the world, we can expect that they will continue to dominate and orchestrate most international trade. At the same time, however, we can expect smaller firms to increase substantially their involvement in international trade due to increased world demand for products and services and to their increased international business skills.

What remain less certain are the specific growth rates of international trade for the world and individual countries and the geographic patterns that international trade will take. Both trends will be influenced significantly by future government policies that either encourage or restrict trade and future changes in the other factors that influence international competitiveness. One possible scenario is that governments will enact policies that will favor their domestic firms at the expense of foreign competitors. In other words, they will try to protect their domestic firms and markets from foreign competitors or try to make their domestic firms more internationally competitive via artificial means such as subsidies. If such actions become widespread, the growth of international trade will be less than it would be otherwise, and trade patterns will be highly distorted. Another scenario is that governments will reduce existing levels of protection and let market forces determine international trade's growth and pattern. In this scenario, international trade would reach continually higher levels and reflect more accurately the true international competitive positions of the nations of the world. The most likely scenario is one that falls somewhere between these other two scenarios. That is, some countries will be reducing trade barriers while others will be increasing them. Under these conditions, trade will increase among the group of countries that reduce trade barriers. In all likelihood, trade will decrease both among the group of countries that increase trade barriers and between them and the former group of countries that will not allow conditions of unreciprocal access. (*Unreciprocal access* means one country is able to export freely to another country while simultaneously restricting its imports from the other country.)

Assuming the third scenario, international trade should increase between North America and Western Europe and between these two regions and most of the major economies of the Pacific Rim region, such as Australia, Japan, Korea, Taiwan, and China. However, increased trade with the last four of these countries will depend on their willingness to lower their existing trade barriers and reduce some of the business practices that are currently considered unfair by the Western nations. Should they do so, the greatest volume and expansion of international trade is likely to involve these Pacific Rim countries.

On the other hand, prospects are fewer for increased international trade between the industrialized countries of the Northern Hemisphere and the developing nations of the Southern Hemisphere. It is not likely that the latter will be able politically to grant greater access to their already comparatively closed domestic markets. Nor is it likely that the industrialized countries will be able politically to continue to grant more favorable access to their domestic markets than they receive from the developing countries. Therefore, the prospects for international trade between the North and the South are less favorable, primarily because of political considerations driven by domestic economic conditions. One potential bright spot in this rather bleak scenario is the North American Free Trade Agreement (NAFTA) among Canada, the United States, and Mexico. Once ratified by the respective governments, NAFTA became the largest single market in the world economy, surpassing the European Community (now renamed the European Union). It is also expected to provide a major economic boost (albeit indirect) to the other Latin countries in the Southern Hemisphere, as the expected surge in Mexico's economy would result in increased trade with its southern neighbors. In addition, discussions have already begun about adding Chile to NAFTA and ultimately in expanding NAFTA to all of the countries in Central and South America to form the Enterprise of the Americas. Should this scenario become a reality, there would be an enormous increase in international business within the Americas.

In addition, we can expect some increase in international trade by the countries in Eastern Europe. Long dominated politically, economically, and militarily by the former Soviet Union, the Eastern European countries have begun to move out on their own in terms of international trade. Hungary, Poland, the Czech Republic, Bulgaria, and Romania have all experienced increased trade with the West and are likely to continue to do so in the future. The main impediment is likely to remain their lack of foreign currencies with which to pay for imports. However, as the exports by Eastern European nations continue to increase, they will earn more foreign currency. And in order to export to these countries' growing markets, more Western firms are willing to accept payment in the form of Eastern European products (instead of the exporter's country's currency) —a kind of product swap arrangement called *counter-trade.*

Finally, there are two very large and powerful countries that clearly have the potential to become much more active and important in international trade than they have been in the past. However, these countries' future involvement will depend largely on political factors, both domestic and international. These two countries are China and India. The impressive emergence of China into the global economy during the 1990s has already been mentioned earlier in this chapter. Its absorption of Hong Kong in 1997 will provide even greater impetus and expertise for further economic expansion domestically and internationally. However, the key question for China remains whether the national government will be able to control China's explosive economic growth and still maintain its historically tight societal and political control. Economic reforms of the 1990s are already causing major population shifts and income disparities within China and increased desires for still additional freedoms. Such freedoms are antithetical to Chinese communism. Something will have to give.

As for India, the world's second most populous nation and four-teenth-largest economy, rapid economic growth on a major scale appears likely to remain a hope rather than a reality. Continued internal political strife, cultural and religious clashes, and burgeoning population growth have continued to hinder India's economic growth and development. In fact, India's rank in terms of world GNP (gross national product) has declined since the 1980s. In addition, highly restrictive international business policies, particularly concerning foreign investment, have discouraged international business from occurring at levels it would have achieved otherwise. Nevertheless, significant opportunities remain for some firms in specific sectors of the economy as the business climate in India improves.

The bottom line is that if markets ultimately follow population, more and more companies will seek their fortune in China and India, the two most populous nations in the world. They are also two of the most difficult and challenging countries in which to do business.

International Investment

The future trends for foreign direct and portfolio investments also look promising. Both types of international investment will continue to be influenced primarily by different rates of financial return and financial risk in all countries. Also continuing to be of major importance will be government policies controlling inward and outward investment flows.

In terms of foreign direct investments, many more firms will have the necessary capital and competitive advantages to invest abroad. In addition, more firms will have to invest abroad in order to remain competitive or to enhance their competitiveness. While most of the largest MNEs (multinational enterprises) in Western Europe and the United States have already established investment positions globally, it is likely that they will seek some expansion and reconfiguration of their positions. In some cases, they will sell some of their existing investments to other MNEs. In other cases, they will expand the basic objectives for their international investments.

The biggest foreign direct investors in the near future will undoubtedly be the United States, Germany, and Japan. Japan now has the capital, confidence, and competitive advantages to increase significantly its international direct investment activity. In addition, Japan will continue to face increasing restrictions on its ability to export to other countries and will need to make direct investments in these countries in order to maintain or increase its market share. Thus, the pattern of Japanese direct investments in the United States, Canada, and Western Europe can be expected to continue as well as Japanese investments in virtually all countries.

Germany will largely be forced to increase its investment in other countries because of the growing high cost of labor in Germany. German wages in manufacturing (including fringes) have become double those in the United States and the highest in the world. German firms have the capital and competitive expertise to substantially increase their operations abroad and are expected to do so particularly in Eastern Europe, the United States, and Japan. They have little choice if they are to match the competitive moves and global market power of U.S. and Japanese firms, their major rivals for world market share.

U.S. firms are also expected to increase their foreign investments, especially in East Asia, Europe, and Mexico. Global competition will drive them to do so in order to hold market share, replace export markets with insider positions, and further develop and refine the current practice of global production rationalization (producing each component wherever in the world it is most efficient to do so). These investments, however, unlike most of those in the past, are more likely to take the form of joint ventures and other types of strategic alliances (rather than the wholly owned subsidiary form so dominantly preferred in the past) because U.S. firms comparatively lack the international expertise and other requirements to go it alone.

Also expected to increase are new direct investments by comparatively smaller firms in the United States, Canada, and Western Europe that will have the increased confidence and need to invest abroad. And finally, firms from several newly industrialized countries (NICs) can be expected to increase their international direct investment activity. Examples of such countries are Korea, Taiwan, Hong Kong, and Brazil.

Other future trends likely in direct investment activity are changes in the types and forms of investments. More firms will utilize joint ventures or other forms of coalitions to minimize risks or to take better advantage of complementary strengths. If trade protectionism increases, more direct investments will be made to displace the previous exports to these countries. If trade protectionism declines, more direct investment will be made to rationalize international production in order to gain international competitiveness. And as international manufacturing activity increases, we can expect a parallel increase in international direct investment activity by the services industries. Likely candidates include the financial services industries (banks, accounting, and insurance firms), the marketing/advertising industries, and the management consulting industry.

We can also expect international investments of the portfolio variety to increase. As world income continues to increase, more people and companies will have additional funds to invest and loan. Companies, governments, and individuals who need funds will increasingly seek to obtain them internationally from these sources wherever they can be obtained at a lower cost or risk. Similarly, governments, companies, and individuals with a surplus of funds will increasingly seek to invest or loan their funds internationally wherever they can earn a higher return or lower risk.

The combination of these trends will result in increased international portfolio investments in the future, as long as governments permit them. The current trend throughout most of the developed world's economies to reduce restrictions on international capital flows appears likely to continue in the near future. What will happen in the distant future is far more difficult to predict. Much will depend on what happens to the growing international debts of the developing nations and the United States.

Other major developments that will have significant impact on international trade and investment are government, corporate, and societal actions concerning the environment. Environmental issues are likely to become preeminent in the twenty-first century at national, regional, and global levels. As some countries and regional economic groups enact more stringent environmental regulations about products and processes, some diversion of international trade and investment is inevitable. In fact, some has already occurred within the European Union and between the European Union and some of its major trading partners. Countries with more stringent standards will be able to reduce or prohibit imports of products not meeting the more stringent standards (and perhaps even acceptable products that were produced using "unacceptable" processes). In addition, some direct investment flows may be diverted into "pollution haven" countries (those with less stringent environmental regulations).

Apart from direct government actions, environmental groups may become more effective at organizing international consumer boycotts of products that damage the environment (the products themselves or the ways in which the products are made or disposed). On the positive side, there will be expanding global markets for environmentally friendly products and processes, waste conversion and recycling methods, and other environmentally oriented industries and companies.

One final but big question mark about future international investment flows concerns the future price of oil. In the earlier discussion about international business patterns in the 1970s, it was pointed out that major changes in the price of oil significantly influenced investment activity throughout the world. As the price of oil quadrupled internationally, a substantial amount of money was diverted from oil-importing nations to the oil-exporting nations (especially to those countries belonging to OPEC). This shift in funds slowed economic growth and investment in the oil-importing nations and accelerated economic growth and investment in the oil-exporting nations.

Because the oil-exporting nations could not absorb all the new funds pouring into their countries, they had to increase their own international investment activity and did so primarily by increasing their international portfolio investments. The net result was a decrease in the amount of funds available for long-term investments in most nations and a resultant slowing of long-term investment activity. Should the future price of oil again experience such a dramatic increase in price, a similar impact on international investment activity could result.

In sum, international business has had a long and diverse history, and its future is likely to be equally long and diverse. What is less certain is the specific pattern it will take in the future. Yet despite this uncertainty, international business is here to stay and will continue to generate an increasing demand for both practitioners and academics in international business. Where these jobs in international business will be located and what the rewards of these jobs will consist of are the subjects of the next two chapters.

CHAPTER 3

FINDING THE JOBS OF THE FUTURE

Under the broadest definition of international business, jobs will be available almost everywhere business is transacted. The basic reason is most firms will be impacted by international business trends. As a result, they will need more employees who understand international trends, their causes, and their implications for the firms' future business strategies and activities.

In addition, there will be more jobs requiring people with much greater in-depth knowledge of international business who also have the very specific skills necessary to conduct business internationally. These kinds of jobs will involve working in an international context on a daily basis and are the types of jobs most commonly associated with international business. (Chapter 5 discusses in greater detail these specific, direct types of jobs in international business.)

PRACTITIONER CAREERS

Geographic Location

By definition and logic, most international business jobs will be increasingly available in the countries most heavily involved in international business. As a result, jobs will be most available in industrialized countries that are already major players in international business such as the United States, Japan, Canada, Australia, and those in Western Europe. In addition, international business jobs will be found increasingly in newly industrialized countries such as China, Korea, Taiwan, Hong Kong, Singapore, Brazil, India, and Mexico. To a lesser extent, international business jobs will be found increasingly in other developing nations in the Pacific Rim, Latin America, the Middle East, Eastern Europe, and Africa (probably in this order).

In virtually all cases, most international business jobs will be located in urban areas, and the biggest percentage of these jobs will be located in each country's largest cities. The reason is the larger metropolitan areas contain the largest number of firms and government agencies and also typically contain the country's biggest firms (the ones most likely to be involved in international activities). Major urban areas also contain the greatest number of service facilities and industries that are likely to be involved in international business, such as seaports, airports, rail and truck depots, warehousing and distribution centers, international customs operations, and financial services firms.

Not all international business jobs will be located in major urban cities, however. Many companies involved in international business are headquartered in much smaller cities and some even in primarily rural areas. Examples include companies such as John Deere and Company in Moline, Illinois; Caterpillar Tractor Company in Peoria, Illinois; Dow Chemical in Midland, Michigan; Michelin Tire Company in Clermont-Ferrand, France; BASF in Ludwigshafen, West Germany; Volkswagen in Wolfsburg, West Germany; and Olivetti in Ivrea, Italy. In addition, many multinational firms operate production facilities in small cities or towns or in primarily rural areas. And finally, smaller cities and towns do have smaller firms that are actively involved in international importing or exporting. Thus, while the greatest percentage of international business jobs will continue to be located in major cities, they will also continue to be available in other locations.

However, it is important to recognize that there is a difference between where international business jobs will be available and where you will be able to obtain them. In other words, the mere fact that a job is available does not mean that you will be able to get it. Many jobs will be restricted by law to be given only to citizens of that country. In addition, most companies prefer to hire citizens of the countries in which they are operating even if there are no legal requirements to do so. Staffing their operations in each country with citizens of that country is almost always less expensive. It is also politically wise in terms of making a favorable impression on the citizens and politicians of that country. In addition, employees brought into a country (from another country) will not know as much about the country as employees who are citizens of the country. As a result, they may not be able to work as effectively or efficiently.

These distinctions are important because they underscore differences in the types of jobs in international business even at an identical location. As an example, consider the French subsidiary of a company headquartered in the United States. In the French subsidiary, virtually all of the employees will be French citizens. Most, if not all, of their primary responsibilities and activities will involve only the firm's operations in France. In a broad sense, they are working in international business because they are employed in a company owned by a foreign investor. However, most of them will not be conducting international business activities specifically unless they are also involved in importing or exporting, for example.

In this same French subsidiary, however, there will probably be several employees who are not French citizens but who are citizens of the United States on temporary assignment from the U.S. parent company. These kinds of employees are called *expatriates* during the times they are working in one of their company's foreign subsidiaries. Expatriates are typically utilized when they possess certain skills or experience that is not sufficiently available in a foreign subsidiary. In addition, expatriates are also utilized by the headquarters company to exercise greater control over foreign subsidiaries and to facilitate the coordination of subsidiaries' plans and operations with those of the larger multinational firm. In these respects, expatriates are involved directly and specifically in international business activities. And to properly conduct their responsibilities, they should be bilingual, bicultural, and familiar with business practices and their firm's operations in France and the United States (and possibly in other countries as well).

However, whatever unique characteristics expatriates possess, they must be beneficial enough to offset the typically lower costs of using local citizens and the benefits that local citizens bring to the subsidiary's operations.

In sum, in virtually all locations of international business there will be different types of jobs. Some jobs will be much more directly involved in international business activities while others will be more involved with local operations. Because of the unique skills and advantages each group possesses, expatriates are most likely to be involved in more internationally oriented types of jobs while local citizens are most likely to be involved in more locally oriented kinds of jobs. Therefore, the location of where you work in international business is not just a question of the availability of international business jobs. It also is a question of your unique qualifications for different types of jobs. For example, depending on the specific skills they possess, German citizens can work in Germany for German-owned firms that do business internationally or work for foreign investors in Germany. They can also work abroad in foreign subsidiaries of German multinational firms or work abroad for non-German companies that do business in Germany or other German-speaking countries.

Industries

On a global basis, some industries are growing very rapidly in terms of international business activity while others are growing less rapidly. At the same time, some industries are not growing at all internationally while a few are actually declining in terms of international activity. In addition, due to shifts in international competitiveness, one country's industry may be declining in international business activity during a time when the same industry in another country is increasing its international activity. Therefore, international business jobs in any industry will be affected by how the industry is doing domestically and globally.

In terms of broad categories of industries, major global expansion is likely to continue at very high rates in electronics, telecommunications, pharmaceuticals, leisure products, and services (particularly financial and information services). Other industries likely to continue to experience good growth rates globally include chemicals, transportation vehicles and parts, health-related industries, tourism, and many consumer products (specialized foods and beverages, toiletries, appliances). All these industries generally involve products that are tied closely to economic development, growth in per-capita income, and changing life-styles. Slower growth can be expected for steel, forest products, many natural resource materials, most fabricated metals, textiles, and apparel.

The primary industries likely to grow most rapidly on a global basis will also be growing rapidly in the United States and Japan and to a lesser extent in Western Europe. In contrast, the slowest growth industries are likely to be declining in importance in this same group of countries but expanding in importance in developing countries. The newly industrialized countries in Latin America and the Pacific Rim will be sequentially moving out of the slower-growth industries and into the higher-growth industries.

Functional Areas

The fastest and biggest growth in international business jobs will probably occur in international finance and accounting. As international trade and investment continue to expand, international finance and accounting jobs will have to expand commensurately in order to obtain, supply, and manage money, to account for transactions, and to provide more accurate information on which to make a wide variety of business decisions. In all likelihood, these two areas also will continue to offer the greatest number of entry-level jobs in international business and the best opportunities for working abroad.

International purchasing and marketing are two other functional areas where more jobs are likely to exist in the future. In order to remain or become more competitive, more and more firms are purchasing raw materials, semifinished products, technology, services, and equipment from foreign suppliers. International purchasing allows the firm to get what it needs at lower prices, better quality, and sometimes both. It may also allow the firm to obtain things it needs that are just not available locally. As more firms recognize these advantages of purchasing internationally, they will need more personnel who can do it well. Viewed from the other side, increased international purchasing creates increased demand for personnel who can sell a company's products or services internationally. It also requires employees who can identify potential customers in foreign markets and who can develop an appropriate strategy to make potential customers aware of the company's products or services and then convince them to buy them.

Another functional area where there will be more international business jobs in the future is international production. While many firms will continue to prefer to purchase what they need from foreign suppliers, there are often advantages for companies to produce by themselves what they could purchase. For example, one major advantage is that the firm gains better control over costs, quality, and availability. It also does not have to share secretive or otherwise important information about the company with suppliers.

There is also a completely different situation in which international production may be needed or beneficial. A firm might not be able to export its product to a foreign country or may face limitations on how much it can export. In either case, one alternative is to establish production facilities in that foreign country, the output of which is sold entirely or primarily in that country.

International logistics is another area where there will be additional jobs in the future. Whenever international trade takes place, products must be physically moved from one country to another. This physical movement of goods involves collecting the goods to be shipped, arranging for their transportation out of the country and into the importing country, and ultimately delivering the goods to the customer's location in the other country. It may also involve arranging for the storage of the goods in the importing country until they can be delivered to the customer. All of this is international logistics, which must be done in a timely and secure manner. As international trade and investment increase, so will jobs in international logistics.

International planning and management are the final areas where jobs in international business will become increasingly available. Increasing international business of all forms will require more people who can plan and manage the international activities of their companies (or their affiliates). In addition, there will be a need even in firms that do not have any international activities. These firms will increasingly need to have planners and managers who understand how international trends may impact the companies' operations in their domestic market (such as import competition, for example).

THE LONG-TERM PROSPECTS FOR INTERNATIONAL BUSINESS JOBS

The long-term prospects are highly favorable for jobs in international business. International business activities will be increasing steadily in amount and variety. More countries, industries, and companies will be involved as well as more locations in each country. More jobs will be directly involved in international business or have occasionally international aspects. More jobs will also be created in industries that support and facilitate international business activities. Finally, additional international business-related jobs will become available in the educational system because of the need to better educate and prepare people for lives in an increasingly internationalized world.

However, it needs to be pointed out again that the existence of more international business jobs does not mean that you will be able to get one. You will have to be eligible, properly prepared, and have the appropriate psychological and motivational attributes.

CHAPTER 4

THE BENEFITS OF AN INTERNATIONAL BUSINESS CAREER

REWARDS OF A PRACTITIONER CAREER

It is not easy to identify ahead of time what any individual will consider pros and cons of a specific career. Job satisfaction is dependent on many different factors, including salary and benefits, social status, employment stability, intellectual and motivational challenges, psychological rewards, geographic location, and the general work environment. Certain factors will be more important to some people than they will be to others. Job satisfaction is also influenced by the alternatives an individual has for employment in other careers. In other words, a person may see many more advantages (and fewer disadvantages) to being a medical doctor than being an accountant but not be able to become a doctor. Finally, job satisfaction depends on the particular preferences of each individual. That is, some people like a high-pressure job, but others do not; some like to travel, but others do not. Therefore, the aspects of a particular career that cause one person to love it may cause a different person to hate it.

These points are worth keeping in mind when reading and thinking about the information provided in the rest of this chapter. The information describing the advantages and disadvantages of a career in international business is drawn from the perspectives of people who generally like their jobs in international business. It is up to you to decide if you have similar likes and dislikes.

A practitioner is someone who actually works in business, either domestic or international, and is either self-employed or employed by some organization. Not included under this definition are educators. Possibly included under this definition are lawyers and government officials who are responsible for economic/business development. However, most of this discussion pertains to those who work in the business sector. In addition, many of the advantages and disadvantages of careers in international business are significantly related to those for careers in business as a whole. For example, salaries in international business are high because salaries in business are generally higher than those in many other careers. Stated another way, there is a certain salary level for business in general and a special salary consideration for people in international business.

Financial Rewards

In all candor, it is the considerable financial rewards from a career in international business that attract many people to this occupation. Senior executives in international business can typically earn salaries exceeding $100,000 a year, and some earn more than $500,000.

The high salary levels in international business result from several factors. The increased importance of international business has created a greater demand for people suitably trained for international business careers, which in itself has brought about rising salaries for people in international business. Second, there continues to be a shortage of people trained for international business, so the increased demand plus the shortage of supply has led to even higher salaries for international business personnel. Third, most big jobs in international business are found in multinational firms, typically the largest, most prestigious, and often the most profitable firms in each country. These firms have the ability to pay higher salaries than most smaller firms. Fourth, most international business jobs are located in major urban cities where the higher costs of living require higher salaries. Fifth, most international business jobs are in financially strong, internationally competitive industries. These industries can afford to pay higher salaries. Finally, many international business jobs require assignments abroad. These foreign assignments involve certain hardships for the people who undertake them—hardships the individuals are normally compensated for by additional amounts of salary or other benefits.

Unfortunately, there are few statistics available about entry-level positions in international business in the United States or elsewhere. The main reason is that there are not many entry-level jobs in international business compared to the number of entry-level jobs in finance, accounting, marketing, and the other functional specializations within business. For the most part, companies hire people initially into one of these functional areas rather than directly into international positions. After several years of proving themselves in a domestic capacity, these people become eligible for jobs with international responsibilities or aspects.

There are even fewer statistics available for salaries for mid-level positions in international business. The main reason is that a high percentage of these jobs are filled by companies' existing personnel rather than being advertised. And because there is less of an organized external job market for these positions, there is less information about them that is publicly available. Therefore, once again the best proxies for international business salaries are the salaries for the functional specializations, even though salaries for the latter tend to be lower than for jobs in specializations that are international in scope.

Finally, available data about salary levels for senior executive positions in international business are also in short supply. At the top level of most companies there may be only a handful of positions that carry the term *international* in their official title. However, most of the top positions have international dimensions and responsibilities even if the word *international* is not an official part of the title. For example, the title *senior vice-president of finance* does not suggest that this position has any international aspects. In all likelihood, however, the position has substantial international aspects, especially if the position is in a multinational firm.

What remains after all of this discussion is the following. There are some fairly good statistics on entry-level salaries in the functional areas of business but not many on entry-level positions in international

AVERAGE ANNUAL SALARY OFFERS FOR
BUSINESS EMPLOYMENT

Bachelor's Degree Candidates
(Data Combined for Men and Women)

By Occupational Title for All Types of Employers	Average $ Offers March 1994
Administrative and Management—Related Occupations	
Accountants and Auditors	$28,371
Banking Occupations	24,600
Business Administration	23,820
Consultants	31,239
Financial Analysts	28,117
Human Resources	24,319
Management Trainees	23,545
Computer and Mathematical Occupations	
Computer Programmers	30,100
Computer Scientists	31,701
Mathematicians/Statisticians	26,674
Systems Analyst	38,371
Marketing and Sales Occupations	
Advertising/Marketing	20,767
Sales	25,421
Brand/Product Manager	25,848

Master's Degree Candidates

Accounting	$32,428
MBA (with 1–2 years' experience):	
Nontechnical bachelor's degree	37,992
Technical bachelor's degree	56,500
Human Resources	39,100
Management Information Systems	33,400
Marketing	47,026

Source: *CPC Salary Survey,* March 1994.

business. There are even fewer good statistics about mid-level salaries in international business and fewer yet about senior-level salaries. The preceding table presents a very widely accepted and publicly available salary statistics for entry-level business positions in the United States, by occupational title for all types of employers. Finally, because the United States generally has the highest salaries in business (compared to other countries), it is reasonably safe to say that business salaries in other countries are likely to be lower than in the United States.

Intellectual and Psychological Rewards

As the old saying goes, "While money is nice, it isn't everything." And, in fact, many people are drawn to international business careers for reasons other than money. One major nonfinancial reason is the intellectual challenge posed by international business. No matter how complicated and intellectually challenging a domestic job is, doing the same job in an international setting is even more complicated and challenging. In international business, there is a greater diversity of people involved. Different cultures want different things, value things differently, and use different methods of achieving their goals. In different countries, identical products may be used in different ways, or different products may be used for similar purposes. What motivates an employee to work hard in one country may be different from what motivates an employee in another country. Some countries place great value on efficiency while others place great value on effectiveness. In some countries, time is very important (if not crucial) while in other countries a more relaxed attitude toward time exists. For all of these reasons, the great diversity of people involved constantly creates intellectual challenges for people who work in international business. They must be able to identify and understand these cultural differences and also be able to determine how to cope with them.

Another intellectual challenge arises from differences in environments and situations encountered in international business. Information that is easily available in some countries is hard to obtain in other countries and may not be available at all in still other countries. Tasks that are easy to perform in some countries may be difficult or virtually impossible to carry out in other countries. For example, arranging for a telephone to be installed in some countries may require more than a year of waiting. Some countries have relatively calm, stable environments while others have very turbulent, unstable environments. In some countries, firms have considerable freedom to conduct their activities as they see fit, while in other countries, firms' activities are highly restricted by laws. Some countries make it easy to take money out of the country while others make it difficult or nearly impossible. Identifying, understanding, and coping with these environmental differences pose considerable challenges to anyone's intellectual abilities.

The great diversity of people and conditions in international business produces a need for creative approaches and solutions. It also frequently requires many changes in the ways businesses must operate if they are to be successful. It also requires changes in the way business people typically think about their country, their business, their products, their production process, their employees, customers and suppliers, and even about themselves. As you learn more about different people and situations and have to confront them, considerable reexamination of yourself, your company, and your country inevitably results. In many cases, you may discover that your firm's or country's way of doing something is not as good as the way it is done somewhere else. Or you may discover that conditions that you have accepted as being somehow unavoidable, such as pollution in cities, are avoidable as you visit some other country's cities and find that they are very clean by comparison. In short, international business forces people to do a great deal of reexamination, not all of which will be pleasant, but all of which will be enlightening and intellectually stimulating.

Motivational Rewards

Trying to overcome the greater intellectual, psychological, and operational challenges of international business is a powerful motivating force in itself. The necessary intellectual gymnastics required, the cross-cultural interactions and experiences involved, and the many related frustrations to be overcome can each be highly motivating both collectively and in their own right. Succeeding under such difficult circumstances is both a motivating force and a motivational reward. Learning a foreign language and how to use a foreign country's transportation system are examples of motivating forces and motivational rewards in international business. And finally, the sheer dynamics of international business is a powerful motivator for many people. Conditions are changing constantly in each country and in the relationships between countries. Nothing is static in international business; everything is dynamic. As a result, there is little chance of becoming bored in an international business career, of knowing all there is to know, or of having experienced all there is to experience.

Cultural Rewards

For many people, the cultural aspect of international business careers is the most important reason they select this field and the most rewarding part of their careers. Rewards are found in learning about other cultures' life-styles, aspirations, ways of thinking, and business practices. Cross-cultural interaction and experiences broaden people's horizons, perceptions, and perspectives. They force a less biased view of one's self, country, and life-style and a greater appreciation and tolerance of different cultures. They force people to redefine their notions of good and bad, better and worse, and many other judgmental criteria. They generate new alternatives to consider and possibly to implement. They allow an increased ability to select the best from what the world has to offer, leading to an enriched life for those who are open to change. There is truly a big and diverse world out there, and no country has a monopoly on all the right answers or even the right questions. We can and should all learn from each other, and having a career in international business is an excellent way to do so.

NEGATIVE ASPECTS

The preceding discussion should not suggest that there are no negative aspects of international business. No career has only good aspects, including international business.

There are often considerable risks in international business, and many times these risks are higher than those in purely domestic business. There are virtually always more uncertainties in international business than domestic business as well as more headaches and frustrations because of the greater complexities. For jobs that require substantial international travel, there are many physical and psychological discomforts associated with being away from your own country and from the frequent inconveniences of international travel itself.

Some people you will have to interact with in international business you may not like for one reason or other because they are so different. Similarly, many situations you will encounter will be uncomfortable or unpleasant for you because they are so different (such as different foods) or because you do not know how to behave.

If you are stationed abroad for a considerable period of time, you may find it difficult to return to your own country or to fit back into the headquarter's operations because you have changed or conditions at headquarters have changed. Or some of the previously mentioned advantages of a career in international business may be considered by you to be disadvantages.

WHO SHOULD SEEK A CAREER IN INTERNATIONAL BUSINESS?

It should be clear that international business careers are not equally suitable for everyone. They are most suitable for people who are curious, flexible, adaptable, observant, and open-minded. They are suitable for people who love challenges and nonroutine situations. They are suitable for people who can handle risk, uncertainty, and frustration. They are suitable for people who are patient, motivated, and self-disciplined. If you possess most of these characteristics, international business is a career for you to consider. If most of these characteristics do not describe you, it is unlikely that international business is the right career for you.

ACADEMIC CAREERS

With very few exceptions, an academic career in international business means a faculty position at a college or university. The fundamental reason is that there are very few opportunities to teach and conduct research in international business at any other level of the educational system or outside the educational system. Therefore, *academic careers* here refers to those at the college or university level.

People choose an academic career for a number of reasons. Perhaps more than anything else, an academic career is a life-style choice. Compared to many other occupations, an academic career has more flexible hours, time schedules, and work loads. Academic careers are also generally less hectic in pace, have less supervision, and are more self-directed. They also tend to be more intellectually stimulating and challenging.

However, pay levels and employee benefit packages are generally lower in academic careers than they are in practitioner careers, and there are fewer international business jobs available in academia than in business. In addition, an academic career requires several more years of education than a practitioner career. Average salaries for business faculty and administrators are presented in the following tables.

Because of these differences, most people will have a definite preference for either an academic career or a practitioner career and will be more psychologically and otherwise suited for one compared to the other. If you have decided on an academic career or have not yet decided one way or the other, you should find the remaining sections of this chapter to be enlightening and useful.

1993–94 BUSINESS FACULTY SALARIES[1] BY DISCIPLINE

	Professor	*Assoc.*	*Ass't*
Accounting	$74,900	$59,700	$55,700
Finance	79,000	62,600	59,600
Management[2]	72,800	57,200	52,600
Marketing	73,400	58,200	54,300
Quantitative Methods	71,600	55,900	50,800
Production/Operations	76,000	59,500	55,100

1993–94 BUSINESS FACULTY SALARIES[3] FOR ADMINISTRATORS

	Public University	*Private University*
Dean	$97,500	$106,200
Assoc. Dean	85,100	92,800
Asst. Dean	59,700	56,800

[1]Salary figures are for a nine-month contract and are the mean salaries reported.

[2]Includes international business

[3]Salary figures are for a twelve-month contract and are the mean salaries reported.

Source: AACSB Salary Survey, 1993

Location of Academic Jobs

There are literally thousands of colleges and universities in the United States alone. They are located in every major city in every state and even in many small towns in primarily rural areas. They include two-year colleges, four-year colleges, universities offering both under-graduate and graduate degrees, and a few institutions offering only graduate degrees. They also include both private and state-supported institutions.

Yet despite the many locations and varieties of colleges and universities, faculty positions in international business do not currently exist at most of them. They are very rarely found in two-year colleges and are somewhat more prevalent in four-year colleges. (However, more positions are being created at both two-year and four-year colleges every year.) As a result, the vast majority of international business faculty positions are currently located in universities offering graduate degrees.

Because most universities serve a particular regional area, you are more likely to find academic positions in international business in regions where there is significant international business activity. And because most international business activity occurs in major metropolitan areas, the universities in these areas are the most likely to have courses, degree programs, research activities, and faculty positions in international business. Notable exceptions include many large state-supported universities that are internationally oriented but are not located in major cities, such as Penn State University, the University of Michigan, Indiana University, the University of Alabama, Texas A & M, and the University of South Carolina. In addition, several prestigious private universities located in small towns (such as Dartmouth University in Hanover, New Hampshire, and Stanford University in Palo Alto, California) are actively involved in international business education.

In most cases, however, the availability of international business faculty positions is positively correlated with the size of the university or the town in which a university is located. Therefore, good hunting grounds for jobs include New York, Boston, Philadelphia, Chicago, Los Angeles, San Francisco, Miami, and Atlanta. They also include the largest state-supported universities in most states and the most prestigious universities, regardless of the size of the city in which they are located.

Rewards of an Academic Career in International Business

The rewards of an academic career in international business begin with the rewards of an academic career in any field. Other rewards pertaining more specifically to an academic career in international business are similar in virtually all respects to those of a practitioner career in international business. In other words, whether you are involved in international business as a practitioner or as an academic, you are likely to find that your job and your life have more diversity, complexity, intellectual and psychological challenges, opportunities for foreign travel and cultural enrichment, and increasingly greater importance to society.

Negative Aspects

All careers have some negative aspects associated with them, and an academic career in international business is no exception. There are fewer universities that offer courses and degree programs in international business than other functional fields in business. As a result, there are fewer faculty positions in international business and fewer places where you can obtain a doctoral degree in international business that best qualifies you for a faculty position.

Only a handful of colleges and universities have an international business department or a tenure and promotion track in international business. For this reason, your faculty position, promotion, and tenure will most likely involve a functional area such as marketing, finance, accounting, or management. As a result, your hiring, promotion, and tenure typically will depend on your professional suitability and performance as viewed by faculty whose primary interests are not international. Therefore, it may be more difficult to get hired, promoted, and tenured if your primary activities are international.

In addition, conducting international research is more difficult and expensive than conducting domestic research, and there are fewer academic journals that regularly publish international business research. Because promotion and tenure usually depend heavily on the amount of research published, it may not be as easy for internationally oriented faculty members to be promoted and tenured as it is for their domestically oriented colleagues.

Before you select your area of specialization, you should carefully weigh the advantages and disadvantages of specializing in international business versus one of the functional fields of business. In order to lessen this dilemma, it should be pointed out that there are considerable advantages to developing a strong expertise in one of the functional areas in addition to a specific expertise in international business. This issue and how to deal with it are discussed in greater detail in chapter 6.

CHAPTER 5

THE SPECIALIZED FIELDS OF INTERNATIONAL BUSINESS

The major types of specializations in international business are essentially the same as those in domestic business. Both kinds of business involve accounting, finance, marketing, purchasing, logistics, production, human relations, planning, research, and management. However, conducting these activities internationally is not the same as conducting them domestically. In most cases, some adaptations must be made in these activities in order for them to be performed successfully in international business.

In addition, all of the major types of business activities are necessary to make international business successful for the firms involved. Failure to devote proper attention to any one of them may cause planned operations not to take place or to be less successful than they could have been. The history of international business is full of unfortunate and unnecessary failures. Many resulted from improperly performing just one specific activity or not performing it at all. Therefore, all business activities must be performed with appropriate adaptations to cultural, legal, political, and economic differences between countries.

Finally, even though you plan to work in international business, in all likelihood you will work primarily in one specific field of international business such as international finance, international marketing, or international accounting. This chapter describes the nature of each of the major areas of specialization within international business. After reading about them, you should have a better idea about what each specialization entails and which specialization most interests you and is most suitable for you.

INTERNATIONAL ACCOUNTING

All companies must keep written records of their operations in order to provide information for their owners, employees, and managers. Such information is also desired by groups outside firms who have some interest in a company's financial well being, such as governments, creditors, suppliers, and customers. These written records serve as a kind of scoreboard of a company's operations, showing both the results of operations and how they might be improved in the future. They also permit comparisons to be made to other companies. And no matter how small a company is, there is a huge amount of information it must deal with on a daily basis.

It is the primary responsibility of accountants to collect, prepare, analyze, store, and distribute numerical information to people who want to know how well a firm is doing. Therefore, accounting is a specialization well suited for people who are good with numbers and who like working with them. It is also well suited for people who are detail oriented and who like fairly structured tasks and work environments.

Within accounting there are four main areas of specialization: financial accounting, managerial accounting, tax accounting, and auditing. Each of them is described, along with its international dimensions.

Financial Accounting

The major task of a financial accountant is preparing financial reports that both summarize and detail the financial position of a firm and the results of its operations for people outside the firm. These reports are used primarily by stockholders, government agencies, the financial community, prospective investors, suppliers, and customers. In doing their job, financial accountants must be concerned with the proper valuation of a company's assets and liabilities, revenues and expenses, and any changes in their amount and value over time.

The international complexities of financial accounting stem from many different sources. Among the most important are different currencies and changes in their values, national differences in inflation rates, national differences in how financial reports are prepared, and national differences in the accounting principles and procedures that are used to generate financial reports.

In preparing the financial reports of a multinational firm headquartered in the United States, financial accountants must consolidate the assets, liabilities, and financial results of the firm's foreign subsidiaries. To do this they must restate the financial records of the foreign subsidiaries that are not prepared in English, U.S. dollars, or according to accounting principles and procedures that are generally accepted in the United States. These tasks are not easily done because they require an in-depth understanding of differences in language, terminology, accounting principles and procedures, and also the specific accounting procedures permitted in the United States for consolidating foreign subsidiaries.

Similar kinds of complexities confront a financial accountant who wants to analyze an unaffiliated foreign company's financial reports. A foreign company's reports usually are not prepared in the same manner as those of U.S. companies. They typically contain less information, often less reliable information, and information that has been prepared in different ways from what is considered generally acceptable in the United States.

Financial accountants must also account for changes in the values of foreign currencies that affect the value of a firm's business transactions. For example, a U.S. firm purchasing equipment from a French company will usually have to pay for the equipment in French francs. If the value of the franc increases by 10 percent relative to the dollar between the time the purchase contract is signed and the payment is made, it will take 10 percent more dollars to get enough francs to pay the French supplier. As a result, the increased cost of the equipment purchase transaction must be accounted for by the accountant. Because a multinational firm does business in dozens of currencies, financial accountants must be constantly adjusting accounts because of changes in exchange rates.

Managerial Accounting

The major role of a managerial accountant is to collect, prepare, analyze, and report accounting information needed for decision making by the firm's management. Therefore, a managerial accountant is primarily internally oriented while a financial accountant is primarily externally oriented. Typical of the types of activities a managerial accountant performs are providing information to management about production input costs; capacity utilization; cost-volume-profit analyses; performance evaluation; and inventory, labor, and equipment utilization. In brief, managerial accountants provide economic information useful in aiding managerial decision making in planning, directing, and controlling an organization's operations.

The international complexities of managerial accounting are numerous and challenging. As one complicated example, consider the job of estimating what it will cost to make a product whose parts will be manufactured in foreign subsidiaries. First, production cost estimates will have to be collected from each subsidiary for each part and then compared to determine who can produce the part at the lowest cost, given a desired quality level. Factored into these cost estimates must be estimates of expected changes in general inflation rates and the specific costs of labor, materials, and other inputs necessary to produce the parts. Second, it must be determined which subsidiaries have sufficient production capacity to produce each part in the desired quantity. Third, costs of getting the parts to the United States must be estimated. Included in these estimates are the costs of packing and shipping the parts, insuring the shipment, storage at the ports of origin and destination, and customs clearances. Also to be considered are tariffs (import taxes that must be paid when the parts enter the United States) and export taxes or subsidies (money paid to or received from the government of the exporting subsidiary's country). Fourth, possible changes in foreign currency exchange rates will have to be estimated. The reason is if one country's exchange rate goes up against the dollar while another's goes down, the dollar costs of importing parts from the former will go up while those from the latter will go down. Finally, the costs of assembling the product in the United States must be estimated, taking into account the same cost factors that the foreign subsidiaries had to evaluate.

If the final product to be assembled in the United States is made from hundreds of parts, such as an automobile or a computer, you can imagine how challenging and difficult a job it is for managerial accountants to calculate an estimated cost for the product. In addition, the estimates are only as good as the sophistication of the accountants who prepare them and the uniformity of the methods used to prepare them. For these reasons, multinational companies must properly train their accountants and utilize common managerial accounting procedures throughout their worldwide operations. These training programs and the design and operation of a common accounting system are also responsibilities of managerial accountants.

Another major international responsibility of managerial accountants involves internationally allocating various shared costs, such as research and development costs, to units of the multinational firm. Managerial accountants also design and operate systems to analyze the performance of foreign subsidiaries and their managements and other international internal information systems. They also provide financial accountants with some of the information they need to prepare their financial reports.

Tax Accounting

In one form or another, all governments tax companies and individuals located within their taxing jurisdiction. As a result, companies need tax accountants to prepare government-required tax reports for the firms and, in some cases, for the firms' employees. The basic responsibility of the tax accountant in these situations is to use every legitimate (legal) means to minimize the taxes owed on the income earned. In addition, many companies utilize tax accountants in a planning function. In this capacity, a tax accountant tries to determine ahead of time how much taxable income may be generated and if there are ways of structuring and conducting operations differently that will result in lower taxable income. Finally, governments need tax accountants to evaluate the tax returns of companies and individuals.

One major international complexity of tax accounting arises from national differences in taxation principles, procedures, and practices. No two governments have identical taxation systems. Some primarily use direct taxes on income to generate government revenue, such as the United States. Other governments primarily use indirect taxes, such as sales taxes, excise taxes, and property taxes. Many developing countries utilize this indirect approach. In addition, the definitions of what constitutes taxable income and tax deductible expenses vary from country to country. As a result of these differences, identical business operations that result in taxable income of 10 million dollars in one country might result in a taxable income of only 5 million dollars in another country. Because multinational firms operate in different countries, their tax accountants must understand thoroughly each country's taxation system. Some important corporate decisions, such as where to locate a manufacturing facility, often depend heavily on these tax considerations.

The biggest international complexity of tax accounting arises when two countries claim the right to tax the income of a company. For example, the United States claims the right to tax the income of foreign subsidiaries of U.S. companies. In addition, the governments of the countries where these subsidiaries are located also claim the right to tax the subsidiaries' income. In these situations, a company faces the possibility of double taxation—having to pay taxes twice on the same income. And if both countries have tax rates of at least 50 percent, the company being taxed could have no income after tax no matter how much it earned. If this were to happen, the business would go bankrupt or not be established at all.

To prevent double taxation, many countries establish tax treaties with other countries, detailing who has what tax jurisdiction, how much, and other legal arrangements. In most of these cases country X will allow country Y to first tax the income of the company, then allow the company to deduct taxes it paid to country Y against the taxes it owes to country X. However, it is always more complicated than this, because what country X considers taxable income may not be considered taxable income by country Y, and so on. It takes very shrewd tax accountants to sort out and solve these international tax problems.

International tax accountants also are called upon to provide information and advice on the legal and tax structure a company should select for itself and its operations. Some companies have moved their headquarters to another country or changed the legal form of their company for tax minimization reasons. Or some companies decide to operate overseas as a branch rather than a subsidiary while others make the opposite decision, depending on international tax considerations and the expected tax impacts on their firms. International tax ramifications also affect the direction, magnitude, and timing of international financial flows within a multinational firm. Under certain conditions it is possible to maneuver income out of a high tax-rate country into a lower tax-rate country. This can be done by altering financial flows and the prices of products and services transferred among different operating units of a multinational firm.

Even if a company does not have overseas subsidiaries but is involved in other ways in international business, it is likely to have some international tax complications. The taxation of its export activities is one example. Some countries provide tax credits or other tax reductions in order to encourage firms to export. Tax accountants should be aware of these opportunities and take advantage of them in order to reduce taxes the company pays on its export profits. They must also make sure that all necessary records are kept and that the firm is in full compliance with all of the other requirements needed to qualify for the tax reduction. Also, they must calculate the tax impact of any financial gains and losses on exports, imports, and money borrowed or loaned abroad that results from changes in exchange rates.

If all of this appears extremely complicated, your perception is correct: international tax accounting is extremely complicated. In fact, it is probably the most complicated area of international business. But because international tax accountants can save companies millions of dollars each year, they are also some of the most highly paid. So if you thrive on complexities, enjoy developing innovative approaches and solutions, and like a big salary, international tax may be the right career for you.

Auditing

Auditing is essentially a control function. One of its primary purposes is to ascertain the validity of financial reports prepared by companies to prevent them from cheating or misleading investors, creditors, and governments. This form of auditing is called external auditing. Another major purpose of auditing is to determine if management's operating and financial controls are being followed, whether they are effective, and whether the company's assets are secure from theft and embezzlement. This form of auditing is called internal auditing. Therefore, auditors are a form of control mechanism serving and protecting the interests of persons both inside and outside the firm. What they look for are significant irregularities in business procedures and practices. And if they find them, it is their responsibility to disclose them.

To conduct their jobs properly, auditors must perform many different activities. Examples of these activities are verifying the amount and value of a company's assets and liabilities, revenues and expenses, and the adequacy of its internal control systems. What makes these activities complicated in themselves is the vast number of assets, liabilities, revenues, and expenses that a large company has and the many different locations where a large company has operations. In addition, most audits must be performed at a very specific time and generally in a fairly short amount of time. They become even more complicated and difficult to do when the company is a multinational firm with operations scattered throughout the world, often in very remote locations.

Some international complexities of auditing arise from different languages. The auditor usually must be able to speak, read, and understand the language of the country where the audit is being done. International auditors must also understand cultural, legal, and business practices in different countries in order to be able to identify irregularities. Even time zones are sources of complexity in doing an international audit. If some important auditing information from Paris and Tokyo is needed in New York at 5:00 P.M. New York time, it is midnight in Paris and 7:00 A.M. the next day in Tokyo. As a result, it is unlikely that anyone will be in the Paris and Tokyo offices to provide the needed information. And if auditors are traveling frequently through different time zones and countries to conduct their activities, they inevitably will suffer mental and physical fatigue and discomfort. But if you want to travel internationally, international auditing is the job for you.

Because of some of the negative aspects of having traveling auditors (or the inability to find enough personnel who are suitably trained to audit internationally), some audit activities are performed by local auditors in the countries where the audits are taking place. Thus, you might be involved in only one portion of a larger international audit. Or you might be involved in training foreign auditors to work with you or review the audit work they have performed for you.

In any form, auditing is a very exacting job with a great deal at stake. If auditors fail to do their jobs properly, a great deal of money and other assets can "disappear" or be otherwise hidden, or a firm might go bankrupt, causing many people to lose their investment or their jobs. And in some countries, auditors can be sued. Therefore, there are many responsibilities riding on the shoulders of auditors in general, and especially international auditors. It is a demanding but necessary and important job worth considering as a career.

Other Career Choices in International Accounting

In selecting a career in international accounting, there are also choices to be made in terms of the kind of organization for which to work. Broadly speaking, there are three major options: public accounting, government accounting, and corporate accounting.

Public accounting involves working for an accounting firm, the largest of which have operations in most countries of the world. Examples include Arthur Andersen, Price Waterhouse, Ernst and Young, KPMG, Coopers and Lybrand, and DRT (Deloitte, Ross and Tomatsu). These large accounting firms conduct external audits for domestic and multinational firms. They also offer to their clients a wide range of international services in areas such as international tax, international information systems, and management consulting.

Government accounting involves working as an accountant for a government agency, such as the Internal Revenue Service (IRS) or the Government Accounting Office (GAO). Government agency accountants typically check private and public sector organizations for accounting compliance with government rules and regulations. As a result, their work primarily involves auditing.

Corporate accounting involves working as an accountant for a company whose main purpose is not providing accounting services to other companies. Corporate accounting encompasses managerial accounting, financial accounting, tax accounting, and internal auditing.

The largest number of accounting jobs and international accounting jobs are in corporate accounting. In addition, most jobs in corporate and government accounting do not require accountants to have passed all the requirements for becoming a certified public accountant (CPA). However, the public accounting firms are well known and highly regarded for their training programs and offer considerable opportunities in international accounting. The senior partners of the large accounting firms also typically earn more than $100,000 per year. In addition, initial employment with a public accounting firm often serves as a springboard for subsequent jobs in corporate accounting, particularly into companies that are clients of the accounting firm.

INTERNATIONAL FINANCE

Finance involves working with money. All businesses must raise money to get started, spend money to operate, and earn enough money to stay in business. In addition, most firms must earn enough money to have surplus funds to reinvest in the business and to pay a financial return to those who have provided funds to the business, such as owners, investors, and creditors. Finally, all of these activities require that someone properly manage the money obtained and its allocation among competing demands.

Conducting all of these functions involving money is the primary responsibility of people who work in finance. And because money is so important to everyone, those who work in finance have to be particularly careful about how they conduct their activities. As a result, finance people are generally expected to be conservative in their outlook and activities. Therefore, finance careers are well suited for people who like to work with money, who are basically conservative in nature, who are astute with numbers, and who can handle the often enormous pressure of being responsible for money.

By definition, international finance involves working with money on an international basis. Funds for initial and subsequent operations are obtained from investors and creditors in different countries. Financial plans are made for the firm's worldwide operations. Existing funds are allocated to the firm's operations throughout the world. Any surplus funds not needed immediately are invested or loaned anywhere in the world where a suitable return can be obtained. And all of the firm's financial operations must be managed in a global context. Therefore, there are many additional international opportunities and complexities to be considered by people who work in international finance. In addition, there are also special skills and knowledge needed for people who work in international finance. Such people can find jobs in banking, securities and bond trading, insurance, and in the finance and treasury departments of companies.

Obtaining Money

To begin a business, some initial funds must be obtained. Typically, most of these funds will come from those who will own the firm (investors), and any additional funds needed will come from lenders (creditors).

There are several ways to obtain funds from investors, the most common being selling them shares of stock in the company. In order for potential investors to be willing to invest in the company, they will need to be convinced that the future prospects for the company are sufficiently good. Convincing them normally requires providing them with detailed projections of the company's future business operations and financial results, usually called an investment prospectus. Similarly, obtaining funds from lenders typically requires a loan prospectus. Therefore, one responsibility of those who work in finance is to prepare a prospectus in such a way that enough people will provide the money needed.

Obtaining investment funds from international sources often requires the information to be prepared in their language and in a manner familiar to them. It may also require providing them with some kinds of information not normally required by domestic investors. In addition, it is often necessary to expend more time, travel, and effort to find and cultivate investors in other countries because they know less about your firm and the related financial opportunities for them. Finally, what they look for in making an investment may be different from investors in your own country. For example, they may be more interested in receiving dividends than in having the value of their stock increase. Or they may be more interested in the return on their investment expressed in their local currency rather than in the currency of the parent company's country. Therefore, obtaining investment funds internationally is likely to be more complicated than doing so domestically. However, a much larger pool of funds is available internationally, so it is often worth the additional effort and adaptations required.

The same considerations and conclusion apply to borrowing money internationally. There are more lenders and loanable funds internationally than there are domestically. And the preferences and requirements of lenders in different countries also vary from each other and from those in your own country. The costs of borrowing money internationally also differ substantially because of differences in each country's interest rates and changes in foreign exchange rates.

For example, interest rates available throughout the world vary from less than 5 percent to more than 100 percent. If only official interest rates are considered, it makes sense to borrow money in those countries where interest rates are lowest. However, changes in currency exchange rates must also be considered because loans normally will have to be repaid in the currency of the lender's country.

If the lender's currency increases in value relative to that of the borrower, the borrower will have to come up with more local currency to repay the foreign loan. Stated another way, if a U.S. company borrows money from a French lender and the French franc increases in value against the dollar during the time of the loan, the U.S. firm will have to have more dollars to repay the French loan. If the differences in the new exchange rates are greater than the differences in interest rates, the initially cheaper loan from France may actually turn out to be more expensive than a loan obtained domestically. And the reverse of this situation is also possible. It may be ultimately cheaper to borrow funds abroad at a higher official exchange rate. This could result if the lender's currency declines in value against the borrower's currency by an amount greater than the difference in interest rates. Therefore, international finance people must take into account more than just differences in interest rates if they want to borrow money at the lowest total cost.

Investing, Lending, and Allocating Money

The flip side of decisions about raising and borrowing money is decisions about investing, lending, and other forms of allocating existing money. Investors and lenders seek uses for their money that will earn the highest rate of return for an acceptable level of risk. In many instances, they will do better by investing or lending abroad than by doing so domestically. However, there are additional complexities and challenges to be overcome.

First, lenders and investors must become aware of financial opportunities outside their country. Many good opportunities are missed simply because investors and lenders are unaware of them. Second, different attitudes are necessary to evaluate properly international opportunities. Too often, good financial opportunities outside the domestic market are simply ignored, being perceived as too risky just because they are outside the domestic market. Or because the international risks are perceived to be much higher, investors might insist on a much higher rate of return than they would expect from a domestic use of their money. However, realities are often different from perceptions. Many international uses of money may offer higher returns at levels of risk comparable to the domestic market, and some may offer higher returns at even lower levels of risk. Third, different skills are needed to evaluate properly international uses of funds because of differences in language, economic and legal conditions, and the financial information provided to potential investors and lenders. Therefore, it is usually more difficult to technically evaluate an investment or lending opportunity abroad than in one's own country.

As a result, there is a need for finance people who are multilingual and who understand political, economic, and social conditions in other countries. They must also understand different accounting, financial, and other business practices of other countries. Analyzing international investment and lending opportunities is the primary responsibility of people called international financial analysts.

Another important job in international finance is allocating corporate funds among the various operating units and activities of a multinational firm. There are virtually unlimited needs for money but limited amounts of money to allocate. Therefore, each company must decide how to best allocate scarce financial resources within the company. Those who work in international finance have major responsibilities for making these decisions. Among many factors they must consider are the different roles and objectives of each operating unit of the company, differences in the future prospects of success for each unit, and the current financial strength and resources of each unit. They must also take into account legal and other difficulties in getting funds into and out of each country, international tax implications, and a host of other considerations involving international competition. In order to make these decisions, people in international finance first must collect and analyze financial reports and future plans from all operating units of the firm. From this information they must then estimate all expected revenues and expenses from operations. If expected revenues are less than planned expenditures, decisions must be made about how and where to get additional money from operations or from other sources. Alternatively, decisions might have to be made about how to limit or reduce expenditures for specific units and activities. This type of activity is called international capital budgeting.

Minimizing Financial Risk

All businesses face risks that can affect their financial results and even their existence. For example, a firm's product may fail, it may not be able to obtain enough money or supplies it needs to produce its products, or it might not generate enough money to pay its creditors. Or it may become technologically obsolete, be sued in court, or may even be taken over by the government. Multinational firms face all these risks in each country where they operate, as well as unique financial risks from changes in foreign exchange rates and government policies regulating international financial flows. Therefore, minimizing financial risks is vitally important to multinational firms and is a major responsibility of those who work in international finance.

In the previous discussions about borrowing money from a foreign lender and importing a product from a foreign supplier, examples of foreign exchange risks were described. It was pointed out that there was a risk that more money might be needed to settle the transactions if the value of the foreign country's currency increased against the value of the domestic country's currency. Therefore, one job of international finance specialists is to predict whether an unfavorable change in exchange rates will occur and, if so, when. If the prediction is that an unfavorable change will occur before the transaction is completed, then the next decision is whether to protect the transaction and, if so, by what methods. There are usually several methods to protect the transaction, many of which are very complicated and all of which involve certain costs to the firm. The international finance specialist must weigh the costs of protecting the transaction against the likelihood and magnitude of a change in exchange rates.

Another kind of international financial risk is that a government may decide to limit or prohibit funds being taken out of the country. In this situation, a firm's foreign subsidiary may be profitable but cannot send money back to its parent or to any other unit of the company outside the country. International finance specialists must then find other profitable uses for the subsidiary's money inside its country. Or if they think that restrictions are forthcoming, they can try to minimize the amount of money going into or earned by the subsidiary and also try to move as much money out of the subsidiary before the restrictions are enacted.

Another situation involving substantial international risk and the need to get money and other assets out of a country earlier than expected is a potential government takeover of a company or one of its affiliates. This type of government action is called expropriation or nationalization. International law recognizes the legal right of governments to take such action, provided that fair compensation is paid to the investors involved. Historically, however, most governments have not paid fair compensation, and some have not paid any compensation at all. To protect firms against these risks, some private companies and government agencies offer insurance policies for nationalization and expropriation. International finance specialists must again weigh the costs of protection against the likelihood of expropriation/nationalization and the potential magnitude of the loss.

International finance specialists must also protect the value of a firm's assets and earnings from inflation in each country. Unless appropriate financial policies can be implemented that minimize or take advantage of inflation's impact on the firm, a firm will lose money in real terms.

International Financial Planning

The previously described international finance activities clearly indicate the need for international financial planning. While each specific activity involves some planning, there is also a need for an overall planning function that transcends and coordinates the planning done for each activity. Therefore, there are jobs in international financial planning at virtually every level of the firm's organizational structure, the most important and prestigious of which is at the top management level. It is the chief financial officer of a company who has the ultimate responsibility for developing, implementing, and monitoring the financial plans, policies, and procedures for all of the company's worldwide operations. Working with and for the chief financial officer are other international finance specialists, each possessing expertise in some specific aspect of international finance or some region of the world. Because of the enormous sums of money they are responsible for, they are very well paid and occupy positions of great importance. The road to these top positions is a difficult and challenging one requiring a great deal of specialized education, training, and experience.

Other Career Choices in International Finance

In addition to choosing a specialization in international finance, you have several choices about the kind of organization you work for. The three major choices are financial institutions, investments, and corporate finance.

Financial institutions include commercial banks, savings and loan institutions, loan companies, credit unions, and insurance companies. Their major activities are obtaining funds from individuals, companies, and other organizations, then loaning these funds to qualified borrowers. Insurance companies also pay out funds to their clients who have insurance claims against them.

Investment firms (stock brokerage firms and investment banks) such as Merrill Lynch, Paine Webber, Smith Barney Shearson Inc., Morgan Stanley, Salomon Brothers, and Brown Brothers Harriman invest the money of individuals, corporations, and other organizations into stocks, bonds, real estate, and other kinds of financial instruments.

Corporate finance encompasses all the domestic and international financial activities of a company described in the previous section. The largest number of jobs in finance are in corporate finance.

In many countries, there are very clear distinctions among these three different types of organizations. However, these historic distinctions have begun to decrease and, in some cases, have virtually disappeared. For example, the biggest financial institution in the United States, Citicorp, conducts all forms of commercial banking through its wholly-owned subsidiary Citibank. Citicorp also offers to its clients virtually every financial and investment service activity they could need. In addition, many large insurance companies have virtually become investment banks because of deregulations that now permit them to invest their funds in a wide range of financial instruments.

No matter which type of organization you work for, there are many jobs in international finance. In fact, the largest numbers of entry-level positions in international business are in finance. In addition, because of increased international business and increased deregulation of financial markets throughout the world, the dominance of international finance jobs among all types of international business jobs is likely to continue in the future.

INTERNATIONAL MARKETING

According to two old business clichés, "Nothing happens in business until someone sells something," and "Every job in business depends on the people in sales." Whether these clichés are totally accurate or not, sales is a vitally important function for all businesses. A company's sales force is on the front line of business competition and is the most direct link between the company and its customers. Yet while sales is the most widely recognized form of marketing activity, it is not the only form. Other important marketing jobs include product design, product packaging, advertising, distribution, market and marketing research, pricing, and other forms of inducing customers to buy whatever a company is selling. And while people generally think about marketing only products, services such as management consulting services, accounting and financial services, legal services, and postal and other forms of communication services are also marketed throughout the world. However, for simplicity, this book will use the term *product* to include both products and services.

In many senses, marketing is a highly creative type of activity. There always appears to be room in the market for new products, improved products, both less expensive and more expensive products, both more simplified and more complicated products, and different ways of packaging and selling products. At the same time, marketing involves much hard work and many frustrations. So if you have a creative mind, like new challenges and hard work, and can live with some frustration, a career in marketing may be just right for you. And if you are exceptionally creative, adaptable, hardworking, and capable of dealing with frustrations and challenges, international marketing is the right career for you.

All of the basic activities of marketing have international dimensions and complexities. If they are not properly understood and taken into consideration, it will be very difficult, if not impossible, to sell a product successfully in another country. In other words, successful marketing of a product in one country does not automatically guarantee success in marketing the same product in a foreign country.

Product Design

From a marketing viewpoint, products should be designed to satisfy customer needs and preferences. Due to differences in these needs and preferences, different versions of a product may be necessary to satisfy different customers. The greater the differences in customers, the more important it will be to offer different versions of the product. Consider the following examples.

In Japan, England, Jamaica, and several other countries, people drive on the left side of the road, while in the United States and most other countries, people drive on the right side of the road. If a car or truck manufacturer wants to sell its vehicles in both countries, it will need to produce some models with the steering wheel on the left side and others with the steering wheel on the right side. In some countries such as the United States, electricity is provided on an alternating current, 110-volt basis. In most other countries, electricity is provided on a direct current, 220-volt basis. Therefore, a manufacturer of electrical products planning to sell internationally should produce two different versions of the product to account for electrical currency differences. Another example concerns product usage. In the United States, bicycles are primarily for occasional leisure use, while in many other countries, bicycles are primarily used for daily transportation. The bicycle's durability and other features desired by the consumers in these different countries require different versions to be sold in each market. And, in some cases, differences in laws require product changes. For example, artificial sweeteners are prohibited by law in many countries, forcing some food and beverage companies to remove artificial sweeteners from the products they can legally sell in other countries.

There are literally hundreds of other differences in countries' and consumers' preferences that require adaptations of product designs and features. Some adaptations are minor while others are major. Because making product adaptations is expensive and complicated, most firms would prefer not having to make them, or at least not having to make many of them. Therefore, a shrewd international marketer will try to design products that require the fewest and least costly adaptations possible while still being acceptable to different consumers.

As mentioned previously in chapter 2, increased environmental concerns, consumer awareness, and government regulations will create new and expanded markets for "environmentally friendly" or "green" products. They will also force adaptations to be made to products that do not meet these new "green" standards. Recyclability and resource minimization (such as energy and materials minimization) are likely to become extremely important considerations in product design. For example, German automobile manufacturers have already undertaken major changes in the design of their cars in an attempt to make them 100 percent recyclable before the end of the decade, and many other companies throughout the world have experienced savings in manufacturing costs by recycling their waste, converting their waste to energy, or by designing products that use less material.

Advertising, Promotion, and Packaging

Making potential customers aware of a product and convincing them to purchase it are the functions of advertising and promotion. The advertising message must reach potential customers and be presented in ways that they can understand and identify with. Otherwise, the promotional campaign will not be as successful as it could be and may even be a total failure. There are many factors to consider in international advertising such as different consumer literacy levels and languages. In some countries, a significant percentage of the population cannot read. In these countries, written advertisements will not be effective in reaching the illiterate segment of the population, and audio and demonstration types of advertisements will be needed. In addition, many different languages are used throughout the world. And within some countries, there are many different languages spoken. Therefore, advertising has to be done in several languages in order to reach a large percentage of the world's population and, in some cases, even a single country's population.

When different languages are involved, a whole variety of translation problems can arise. A product's name in one language may have a different meaning in another language, and potential consumers in one country may be confused or amused by what a foreign product's name means in their language. Or a poorly done foreign language translation of an advertising slogan or message may be equally confusing, humorous, or even insulting to consumers in a different country.

Advertising and promotional campaigns usually must also be adapted to take into account different cultural values and differences in laws. Comparative advertising is illegal in some countries and considered impolite, rude, or unethical in others. Certain products are not legally allowed to be advertised publicly in some countries, or, if permitted, must be done in a manner socially acceptable to that country. Certain types of advertising popular in one country may appear silly or pointless in another country. For example, the use in advertisements of dogs or other animals considered pets in one country is likely to have a different meaning in countries where these animals are eaten as food. Using price discounts as a promotional technique may work well in some countries but be perceived as an indicator of poor quality or product deficiency in another country.

It is also important to consider changing the packaging of a product when selling it in a different country. For example, different colors carry special meanings or evoke certain feelings in each country. In the United States, the color white symbolizes purity and cleanliness (among other things), but in some Asian countries, white symbolizes death. It would not be wise to sell pharmaceutical products in packages with colors that symbolize death. Each country also has numbers that are considered lucky and unlucky. The number 13 is considered unlucky in the United States, while the number 4 is considered unlucky in Japan. It is not wise to sell products packaged in quantities that are considered to be unlucky. In countries where incomes are very low, products may have to be packaged in smaller quantities in order to be sold, such as individual sticks of chewing gum rather than a pack of 10 sticks. In many countries, the elaborateness of the package is considered to be an indication of the quality and prestige of the product. In these countries, more ornate and fancy packaging may be designed. In countries where illiteracy is prevalent, written labels and instructions may not be effective. In these situations, the package and any enclosed instructions may need to utilize pictures rather than words so that consumers can know what is in the package and how to use it properly.

Increased environmental concerns and regulations are also certain to affect packaging. Less packaging will be used in the future, and greater emphasis will be placed on packaging that is recyclable. Companies whose products or manufacturing processes meet government environmental standards will be able to advertise these certifications on their packaging (such as the European Union's green dot.)

In sum, companies that wish to market their products successfully in other countries need to consider modifying their advertising, promotion, and packaging practices in addition to modifying their products.

Distribution Channels

Distribution channels are the means by which products get from the manufacturer to the ultimate customer. Some distribution channels are short and direct, from manufacturer directly to customers. In most cases, however, they are longer and indirect, utilizing the services of wholesalers and brokers and, in the case of consumer products, retailers.

From a marketing standpoint, channels of distribution are important because they affect the final price the customer pays for the product, the availability of the product to the customer, and, in many cases, the image of the product. As a result, improper channel selection can result in a firm's products not being available in sufficient quantities, not being available to all potential customers, not being affordable to many customers, or not being perceived as desirable by many customers. In marketing products in other countries, channel selection is even more complicated and important because of the geographic distances involved and differences in laws, business practices, and cultural behavior.

In some countries, products cannot be sold directly to customers. In other countries, the manufacturer cannot utilize one distributor exclusively or force a distributor to sell only its products and not the products of other firms. Distributors may have to be bribed to distribute the firm's products or be given an inducement other than an earned commission on the products they handle for the manufacturer in some countries. In most countries, distributors sell only to specific kinds of customers or in specific geographic areas while some distributors will refuse to distribute a product if it is also to be handled by other distributors they do not like or respect. Many countries can use only specified (approved) distribution channels for certain products. And in most countries, there are unique procedures between manufacturers and distributors and between distributors and customers that must be followed if a product is to be sold successfully.

For all of these reasons, international marketing specialists must carefully investigate distribution practices and laws in each country before trying to sell there. They must also carefully evaluate all potential distribution channels and distributors before embarking on a course of action. The choice of channel and distributor should be consistent with the customer base the manufacturer is attempting to reach, at least to the extent it is possible to do so.

Pricing

In any business, the correct pricing of a firm's products is vitally important because it affects the quantities sold, the revenues received, and the profits earned. Pricing a product too high can result in significantly fewer quantities being sold and potentially less total profit being earned even though the profit margin is high on each product. Alternatively, pricing a product too low can result in insufficient profit being earned even if huge quantities of the product are sold. Therefore, both the costs of producing and distributing the product and the effects of prices on the quantity sold are important considerations in determining the proper prices of products. Pricing specialists are called upon primarily to evaluate the costs of distribution and the likely market response to various pricing alternatives.

In international marketing, there are many more cost factors to be considered and evaluated than in domestic marketing. First, there are additional costs to be considered if the product is being exported, such as tariffs and international shipping, packaging, and insurance costs. Even if the product is manufactured in the foreign country where it is sold, there will still be foreign distribution and advertising costs, product and packaging adaptation costs, and warranty costs to be considered. Failure to consider adequately these additional costs may lead to pricing a product too low.

In addition, there are many more market-related factors to be considered internationally. In some countries, there may be intense competition that demands lower prices than those that can be charged in countries with less competition. In many countries, there are government price controls on products that limit the prices that can be charged and any increases in existing prices. In some countries, customers perceive low-priced products to be inferior, defective, or low status. In all countries, people's income and their ability to borrow influence how many products and how expensive a product they can buy. And in many countries, tariffs (import duties) are based on the price of the product being imported or the economic necessity of the imported product. In these situations, tariffs usually increase significantly the final price of expensive luxury items. All of these pricing complexities generate additional demand for international pricing specialists. Without their special international expertise, international sales and profits will be less than they could be. Even worse, a company may be found guilty of violating a country's laws.

Sales

All businesses need people to actually sell their products. A successful career in sales requires liking a significant amount of travel and excelling in person-to-person interaction. Successful selling also requires high degrees of patience and persistence and an ability to know what customers need, want, and can afford. People in sales must also understand consumer behavior in general and any special peculiarities and preferences of existing and potential customers. And in many instances, salespeople must also be able to sell their ideas and plans to people in their own firms—when a new product needs to be developed, an existing product needs to be changed, or when other changes are necessary to sell a product more successfully.

Selling a product in a different country requires all of these qualities but at higher levels of complexity and degree. Consumers' behaviors, needs, and preferences vary from country to country. Some consumers prefer a direct, aggressive sales approach while those in another country may find this approach rude, obnoxious, and unacceptable. Consumers in one country may not buy from someone they do not know well or do not like while those in another country may not care as long as the product is a good value. In many countries, body language and other forms of nonverbal communication are very important in selling but are relatively unimportant in other countries. And in virtually all countries, successful selling requires the salesperson to be able to speak the language of the customers.

A salesperson covering a large number of countries must become an expert for each country, a truly formidable task. As a result, a high percentage of sales jobs in foreign countries are given to employees of the firm who are citizens of those countries. But even in these situations, headquarters's marketing personnel need to train foreign salespeople and to help plan, coordinate, monitor, and assist in their activities. So if you are good at languages, are socially adaptable, like daily challenges and personal interaction with many different kinds of people, and like to travel, you may want to consider a career in international sales.

Marketing Research and Planning

The complex variety of international marketing activities underscores the importance of marketing research and planning. An enormous amount of specialized information is needed to make good decisions about product design, packaging, promotion, distribution, pricing, and sales techniques in each country. International marketing research provides this needed information. Marketing researchers must identify economic, political, social, and demographic trends throughout the world and in each country. They must also identify the implications of these trends for their firms' existing and future marketing strategies. They need to examine many different published sources of information and also conduct research of their own, including surveys of customers, distributors, retailers, and their own sales forces.

Once information has been collected, including input from the sales force, a marketing plan must be developed for each product and country and for global operations as a whole. This is the responsibility of the international marketing planners. Competitive conditions and corporate objectives in each market must be considered as well as how they affect each other. Financial budgets for all marketing activities also must be developed. Finally, discussions must be held with production, logistics, and finance managers to coordinate all the necessary activities that will make the marketing potential a business reality.

Other International Marketing Career Considerations

The preceding international marketing activities have been described from the perspective of a company that manufactures a product. However, these same kinds of activities are conducted by other types of organizations, including advertising companies, export management companies, agricultural co-ops, distributors, retailers, charitable organizations, and even government agencies. Therefore, careers in international marketing can be found in a wide range of organizations, including some that are not in business to earn a profit. However, the largest number of jobs in international marketing are in the manufacturing sector.

In addition, most international marketing jobs are given to persons with several years of domestic marketing experience. Therefore, you should be prepared to work in domestic marketing for several years before being considered qualified for an international marketing position or assignment.

INTERNATIONAL PURCHASING

All firms purchase equipment, supplies, and materials needed to produce their products. Normal purchasing considerations include quantity, quality, price, financing terms, delivery schedules, and after-sale service. The goal is to obtain what the firm needs when it is needed at the best terms available.

In an increasing number of situations, this goal can be best achieved by purchasing from a foreign supplier. Gone are the days when U.S. firms were the only good sources of supply. In today's and tomorrow's world, there will continue to be firms in other countries that are competitive in all respects to U.S. suppliers and, in some cases, even more competitive. Therefore, the importance of international purchasing activities and expertise will continue to increase.

In most respects, international purchasing activities are the opposite of international marketing activities. For example, instead of learning where in the world there are good customers for a product (international marketing), international purchasing involves learning where in the world there are good suppliers of a product. Or, instead of having to figure out how to sell to a foreign customer, international purchasers have to figure out how to buy from a foreign supplier.

Several other factors complicate the job of an international purchaser. Because of the distances and different laws involved, international delivery is likely to take longer and be more complicated and expensive than domestic delivery. International shipments are also subject to strikes and other delays (such as customs) at both the port of exit and the port of entry. Therefore, more lead time may be necessary in placing an order. Also, problems with the shipment or the material shipped are more difficult to resolve when the supplier is in a foreign country. Therefore, it is important to more carefully evaluate a foreign supplier. In addition, reordering on short notice from a foreign supplier is also more difficult. Ordering and reordering are also often complicated or made impossible by the existence of quotas that limit the amount of a particular product that can be imported during a year. Foreign suppliers also typically require that they be paid in their own currency, so international purchasers must be familiar with exchange rates and their expected movements. And, in some cases, wars, natural disasters, and other types of major disruptions in a foreign country prevent suppliers from being able to produce and deliver their products—a risk that purchasing domestically does not have.

In sum, international purchasing has its own complexities, risks, and challenges that are not too dissimilar from those of international marketing. As a result, international purchasing requires people with specialized international business skills. They need to be able to find and evaluate foreign suppliers, be familiar with international logistics and related complications, understand exchange rates and foreign business practices, be aware of foreign political and economic developments, and be creative in avoiding problems and solving them if they arise. At the same time, it is likely that international competition will continue to force companies to find new and better sources of supplies. It is also likely that foreign suppliers will continue to enhance their competitiveness. Therefore, international purchasing is likely to increase in importance and bring with it increasing demand for international purchasers.

Other International Purchasing Career Options

In addition to purchasing for a manufacturing firm, there are other career options in international purchasing. Many retailers and wholesalers purchase products internationally to sell in their domestic markets or in other foreign markets. Some government agencies also purchase products and services from foreign suppliers. And there are companies that specialize in importing products for other companies. Some of these importers are large corporations, but many of them are small, entrepreneur firms.

Because there are so many companies that want to sell their products, it is comparatively easier to buy internationally than to sell internationally. Therefore, it is also relatively easier to succeed in international purchasing than in international marketing, but the pay is generally lower.

INTERNATIONAL PRODUCTION

Production is a process involving the physical transformation of raw materials and other inputs into semifinished and finished products. Some production processes are large in size and complexity while others are small and simple. Some require extensive skill while others require relatively little skill. International production tends to be large and highly complex and to require extensive skills.

International production involves producing a product or part of a product (called a component) in a foreign country. As a result, it requires managing and training foreign workers and utilizing production processes and technologies that are suitable for the foreign location. It usually involves working with new suppliers. It also entails complying with all the laws of a foreign country and often managing the foreign facility in different ways from its domestic facility.

The most complicated form of international production results from a strategy called international production rationalization (IPR). In simplest terms, the objective of IPR is to produce each component and subassembly of a product in the countries where it is most efficient to do so and assemble the final product where it is most efficient or important to do so. Each component must be produced to exacting specifications so the final product can be assembled without problems. Production and delivery schedules must be carefully coordinated so that every part arrives on time for final assembly. If all goes perfectly, the company can have the lowest-cost product available anywhere in the world. However, there are hundreds of things that can and often do go wrong in IPR and even in much less complicated forms of international production.

Foreign employees can be one source of production problems if they have different work attitudes and work patterns. They may not be accustomed to working as hard, as long, or as regularly as employees in the firm's home country. If so, they may be less productive, and the production process may be less reliable. They may also demand or be legally entitled to certain benefits or treatment not offered to employees in the firm's domestic plants, increasing the cost of production. On the other hand, they may be more productive, loyal, and in other ways better than the employees of the firm's domestic plants. If so, labor management problems and labor costs may be lower abroad. Other international production problems can result from not having as many good local suppliers in the foreign country; not having as good transportation, power-generating, or communication systems; and having to comply with a whole set of different laws.

Despite all the potential problems, international production is becoming more common and diverse. Once again, the powerful forces of increased international competition are the reason behind the trend. To better service foreign markets and even their domestic markets, more and more companies have had to become involved in international production. With this trend comes an increased demand for engineers, production supervisors and managers, and production planners who can cope with the international complexities and challenges of producing in a foreign country.

Other Careers in International Production

Besides working abroad in production or being involved in the management of foreign production, there are careers involving international production in your own country: working in production for a foreign investor. While this type of career is not as international as the other types described, it can still be quite international in many ways.

Foreign investors typically bring with them foreign technologies; production processes and practices; and often production engineers, supervisors, and other technical personnel. You will be better prepared to work in this kind of environment and with this kind of personnel if you have some understanding of the culture and language of the foreign investor. Even if there are not many foreign personnel in the company where you work, there are still foreign personnel in the company's parent firm who will probably visit your company and have some interaction with you. And as a part of the larger foreign firm, your firm will be managed as part of its global operations. So the more you understand international business and international business operations, the better you will understand what your company is doing and why it operates the way it does.

There are also companies that provide advice and other forms of international manufacturing assistance to other companies. For example, they arrange and supervise contracts with foreign companies to do manufacturing for another company, develop arrangements to share production facilities in a foreign country, or facilitate the international transfer of production technology.

A rapidly emerging form of this kind of manufacturing technology transfer is pollution abatement and waste-treatment technology. Companies such as Waste Management and Brown and Ferry are helping companies throughout the world find new ways of reducing water and air pollution, recycling their waste, or finding more efficient ways of disposing of their waste. Similarly, multinational firms are identifying environmentally best practices being followed within their worldwide operations and then encouraging other units of the firm to adopt similar practices. If costs can be saved in the manufacturing process in terms of inputs, outputs, and waste, competitive advantages can be gained, litigation avoided, and public relations improved. The demand will increase for production engineers and planners who can meet these challenges internationally.

INTERNATIONAL LOGISTICS

Doing business requires the physical movement of materials and products from one place to another, such as from suppliers to manufacturers and from manufacturers to customers. Decisions must be made about the scheduling and timing of shipments, the means of shipment (by truck, plane, or ship), the method of shipment (by container or individual package), and the costs and other terms of shipment. These and other related decisions constitute the specialization known as logistics.

In international business, logistics is more complicated than in domestic business. One frequent reason is the greater geographic distances involved, such as moving products from the United States to India, Australia, or South Africa. In most cases, the greater the distance shipped, the longer the shipping time and the greater the shipping costs will be. In addition, provisions must he made for possible strikes or other events that may delay or prevent shipments in all countries involved in the transportation of goods. Other complications arise from the many different national laws regulating the transportation of goods within each country and between countries. For example, foreign airplanes and ships are allowed to transport goods into the United States but are not allowed to transport them between locations within the United States. As a result, arrangements must be made with a domestic company to transport the goods to or from a foreign shipping company. International shipping also requires the preparation of additional shipping documents such as special documents required by customs agencies in the exporting and importing countries.

Customs and other inspection delays also increase the time it takes to transport goods. Goods shipped internationally often must be specially packaged because of differences in local laws, shipping practices, and transportation vehicles and methods. They also usually involve more physical handling, storage, and special treatment than goods shipped domestically, all of which increase the costs and complexities of shipping internationally. And if shipping delays or other problems in shipping occur, such as damage or breakage, it is usually more complicated to solve problems or, if necessary, settle claims with foreign shippers than with domestic shippers.

Because of all these complexities and the increasing volume and varieties of goods shipped internationally, there will continue to be increasing demand for international logistics experts in firms that buy or sell internationally.

Other Career Opportunities in International Logistics

There are many jobs in international logistics in firms that are involved directly in international shipping, storage, and the other activities involved in moving other companies' goods out of one country and into another. Examples include transportation companies that transport goods by air, by land, or by water and companies that provide storage for goods in transit. Other types of companies include freight forwarders and import/export management companies that arrange the international shipping and storage of goods for other companies.

INTERNATIONAL HUMAN RELATIONS

The human-relations (H-R) function in an organization involves the human dimension of operations. It encompasses hiring and firing; employee education and training; evaluation of employee performance; management-labor relations; and employee compensation, motivation, promotion, and allocation. It is a career that is largely internal in scope and involves working with people and people-related concerns. If this sounds enticing to you, you should consider a career in human relations.

International H-R jobs are found almost exclusively in multinational firms and other types of multinational organizations. The simple reason is that these types of firms have large numbers of foreign personnel who work for them, and there are also many foreign assignments and responsibilities for their personnel. Therefore, there are three basic types of international H-R responsibilities. The first deals with foreign personnel in their own countries, such as Japanese employees who work for IBM in Japan. The second deals with international assignments of personnel, for example, when a U.S. employee of IBM is assigned to IBM's Japanese subsidiary or when an employee of IBM Japan is assigned to IBM's U.S. operations. The third deals with worldwide policies and practices and how to keep all H-R policies in harmony and under control, or at least to the extent it is possible to do so.

Foreign H-R responsibilities include coping with different needs and characteristics of people who work in the firm's foreign operations. Examples include training and motivating personnel to do their jobs in the way the company needs the jobs performed and keeping these employees productive and happy. Because of differences in cultures and employment laws, it is usually necessary to utilize different employment practices and policies in each country. Designing appropriate ones for each country is one aspect of international H-R.

Another major aspect is preparing personnel for international assignments and responsibilities, especially those who have not had them before. There are many things these people must become prepared to deal with intellectually, physically, psychologically, and culturally. If they are assigned to a foreign country, they usually must also be given additional financial compensation and other perks to compensate them for working and living in a foreign country. In addition, they must also become prepared for reentry into their own country, especially if they have been abroad for several years. Designing these preparation and compensation systems is the responsibility of those who work in international human relations.

Finally, at company headquarters there are international personnel-coordinating and global responsibilities. These responsibilities involve monitoring and evaluating personnel policies, practices, and developments at all locations, domestic and foreign. Whenever possible, some uniformity among H-R systems in all countries is encouraged and implemented. In addition, the headquarters's staff tries to identify the best and most promising managers throughout the world so it can place them in higher positions in the global organization. The career path to these headquarters positions is a long one, typically requiring previous overseas experience and international responsibilities of a significant nature.

Other Career Options in International Human Relations

One alternative to international H-R jobs in multinational companies is jobs in companies known variously as executive search firms, executive recruiting/placement firms, and occasionally as headhunter firms. Their role is to help locate personnel suitably qualified for international jobs in their clients' companies, such as Korn and Ferry and Spencer Stuart. Another option is in companies that provide training for other companies' personnel who will have international assignments or responsibilities. Many of the large management consulting firms, such as McKinsey and Booz Allen, provide this kind of service for their clients. Another alternative is in organizations other than companies that have international activities such as the United Nations, certain government agencies like the State Department, world health organizations, and certain charitable or philanthropic organizations such as C.A.R.E. or the Ford Foundation.

INTERNATIONAL PLANNING AND STRATEGY

To improve the probabilities of future success, businesses develop plans and strategies. Plans give signals to everyone in the company about the future activities and priorities of the company and establish standards against which future performance will be measured. The planning process itself forces everyone to think concretely and specifically about the future and is a way of achieving internal consensus about the direction of the firm. Strategy translates the plans into specific action formats, showing how a firm intends to transform its plans into realities. The planning and strategizing processes are the essence of scientific reasoning and management because they imply that future outcomes can be influenced by the actions the firm takes. In short, they suggest that the firm can control some of its destiny.

In international business, planning and strategizing are more difficult but even more important than in domestic business. They are more difficult because there are more factors to predict and more factors that cannot be controlled. They are more important for the same reasons. Some planning and strategizing activities take place in each functional specialization of international business. However, there is a need for developing an overall plan and strategy for the company, and these activities must be done at the corporate headquarters level.

The task first involves evaluating the plans and strategies for each division and activity of the worldwide organization and making difficult decisions about the appropriateness of each of them. Next, plans and strategies must be considered from an interactive perspective: how will the plans and strategies of each operation impact those of other operations? Then, even more difficult decisions must be made about resolving conflicting plans and strategies. Finally, all remaining plans and strategies must be prioritized because of financial, personnel, and other constraints. It is a time-consuming and very difficult process, one that demands people with a truly global perspective, high analytical and reasoning abilities, and an ability to make difficult and important decisions.

Other Careers in International Planning and Strategy

The vast majority of the jobs in international planning and strategy are found in businesses that operate internationally. However, some of these jobs exist in firms that aspire to operate internationally. Others exist in government agencies and other nonbusiness organizations that have or aspire to have international activities. There are also many of these jobs in management consulting firms and companies that provide management services to other firms, such as accounting and law firms.

INTERNATIONAL MANAGEMENT

In the most basic terms, management involves putting together all of the separate activities of a business function in a cohesive, integrated manner. At the highest level, it does this for all the separate functions of the business. Management positions have considerable authority and responsibility—authority and responsibility that increase at each level of the organization. Management positions also have high degrees of stress that also increase at each management level. Therefore, management positions are suitable for those who like authority and responsibility and who can deal with pressure and stress.

International management is even more difficult and stressful than managing a domestic operation or firm. There are greater complexities, uncertainties, and risks involved and fewer factors and events that can be controlled. Successfully managing an international operation is difficult enough. Successfully managing a multinational firm is the ultimate challenge for, and test of, anyone in business. People who reach this lofty level have already proven themselves in a wide variety of activities, locations, and situations. In this sense, they are the cream that has risen to the top.

Being a successful international manager requires technical and international skills well above average. It also requires considerable breadth and depth of preparation and experience and the ability to get the best performance out of everyone in the organization, regardless of their duties and location. As a result, there are really no entry-level positions in international management. You have to work your way into them.

Other Careers in International Management

International managers are needed in every organization that has international activities. Other jobs in international management exist in firms that provide international management services to other companies, such as management consulting firms, accounting firms, law firms, and import/export management firms. However, a significant amount of preparation, training, and experience in international business is necessary to get these jobs and to be successful in them. There are no real shortcuts to getting these jobs. However, the better prepared you are for them, the more likely you are to get them sooner.

OTHER CAREERS RELATED TO INTERNATIONAL BUSINESS

There are many other careers related to international business that have not yet been described. One of the largest is international law. Preparation for a career in international law is very different from other careers in international business, in virtually all cases requiring a law degree and preferably one in international law. The careers and life-styles of international lawyers tend to be different from those of international business practitioners, particularly if they work in a law firm instead of a company. However, like international business practitioners, international lawyers must also consider and deal with much more complicated factors and circumstances in doing their jobs than those who work in a domestic context.

Other related careers involve international research and political risk management. Virtually all firms in international business conduct some kind of international research, and there are also companies, such as Business International, that specialize in providing this kind of research to other companies. And because of the importance of governments to international business, there are also many companies that hire people to assess political changes and the related business risks to their companies. There are also a growing number of companies that provide political risk analysis to other companies, such as Kissinger and Associates. Political risk analysts typically have political science training and have learned to apply this training in a business context.

In sum, there are many specializations in international business and virtually unlimited opportunities for those who are properly prepared. How you can become properly prepared is the subject of the next chapter.

CHAPTER 6

PREPARING FOR AN INTERNATIONAL BUSINESS CAREER

There is no simple, magical method of preparing for a career in international business. Proper preparation is really a lifetime process involving many different steps and experiences beginning as early as childhood. Some take place in the formal educational system while others occur outside it. Some can be completed in your own country while others require an international setting. All of the steps and experiences are useful, and some are crucial; having more experiences is better than having fewer.

CULTURAL EXPERIENCES

One extremely valuable type of cultural experience is international travel. The more countries you visit, the broader the perspective you gain. However, when visiting foreign countries, it is important to explore areas that are not on the normal tourist's itinerary in order to observe the real living and working conditions in each country. In general, it is much more educational to stay in lodgings and eat in restaurants that are not frequented almost entirely by tourists. Using public transportation whenever possible is also enlightening and much less expensive. It is also beneficial to negotiate an informal tour of the city and countryside with a local taxi driver, asking the driver to show you some of the nontourist areas.

While the number of countries you visit is important, it is also important to spend an adequate amount of time in each country. In other words, depth of experience is as important as breadth. A whirlwind tour of six countries in five days is not likely to be a very enlightening experience, other than learning why you would not want to do it again. Therefore, the longer you can stay in a country, the more you will learn about things that will be really useful to you.

While one of the main benefits of international travel comes from interacting with foreign people, you do not have to travel internationally to have such interaction. Many opportunities exist to meet foreign people in your own country, and you should take advantage of as many of these local opportunities as possible. Interacting with citizens from foreign countries who live, study, or work in your community is an excellent and relatively inexpensive way of learning about other cultures. Once you look for them, you will probably be surprised to find out how many citizens from other countries live in or visit your own community. For example, the owners and operators of many international restaurants are natives of the countries whose cuisine they feature.

Citizens of other countries can also often be found working in local firms owned by foreign investors. In addition, many cities have organizations, such as international visitor councils, that try to arrange meetings between foreign visitors and local inhabitants, including home visits and home stays. Other organizations arrange local housing for students from other countries while others sponsor cultural events pertaining to foreign countries, such as a German Oktoberfest or a French Bastille Day. At such events, chances are good that you can meet some citizens from the featured country in addition to being able to learn something about the country's culture and possibly its food.

In addition, in many cities there are organizations whose purpose is to bring together people interested in a particular country, such as the Alliance Française for France, the Goethe Institute for Germany, the U.S.–Korea Society, and the U.S.–Japan Society. Becoming affiliated with such organizations can be an excellent way to meet people from, and learn more about, these countries. Finally, do not neglect opportunities to learn vicariously about other countries by seeing foreign films shown in your community. Chances are also good that you will be able to meet people from these countries at the movies.

FORMAL EDUCATION

The formal education system offers many opportunities for you to obtain the outlook, background, and operational skills necessary for a career in international business. Properly preparing yourself for such a career involves taking advantage of as many of these opportunities as early and frequently as possible. However, do not despair if you have already missed some of the possible opportunities. It is almost never too late to get started.

Primary and Secondary Education

In primary school, there is little choice about the curriculum to which you are exposed. At best, opportunities may exist for some foreign language training; for some international content in courses about history, social studies, and geography; and for some exposure to foreign cultures and foods on special international days.

In secondary school, the first real options emerge, particularly in the last few years when there are elective courses. Courses about world history, world politics, international economics, and foreign languages are examples of electives worth selecting. In an increasing number of enlightened high schools, some of these courses may be required. Most people currently working in international business careers had their initial exposure to international topics during their secondary school days, and it was this initial exposure that sparked their continuing interest in international events and experiences.

Undergraduate Education

At the undergraduate level, opportunities abound for developing an international awareness, background, and outlook. Most good undergraduate programs offer a wide range of required and elective courses that are international in scope. Examples include courses about world history and the history of different regions or countries of the world, world geography, comparative political science, cultural anthropology, comparative religion, international economics, international business, foreign languages and literatures, and many other courses about specific areas of the world (typically referred to as area studies courses). All of these courses are good preparation for a career in international business and provide the breadth of knowledge you will ultimately need in your international business career. They also usually help you decide which geographic area of the world you are most interested in (or suited for) in terms of your future specialization.

While it is helpful to have already developed some foreign language ability before entering undergraduate school, it is very important to develop and enhance your foreign language ability during your undergraduate program regardless of your major. Ideally, you should take four years of language training in a specific foreign language, and foreign language courses focusing on business terminology are especially useful. And whenever the requirements for the degree you are pursuing permit options that include internationally oriented courses, take every one you can. At the undergraduate level, breadth of exposure is generally better than depth.

Many undergraduate programs also offer opportunities to spend a semester or year abroad or have shorter-length, study-abroad programs. These kinds of opportunities are extremely valuable preparation for a career in international business, and you should take advantage of at least one. Even if your school does not offer these programs, many other schools offer such programs on an open enrollment basis. Study-abroad experiences permit you to continue your studies while being immersed in a foreign cultural setting and are an excellent way to achieve multiple goals simultaneously.

Several majors at the undergraduate level are useful, but some are likely to be more useful than others. In addition, much depends on whether you plan to subsequently get a graduate degree. Generally speaking, the most useful major for a career in international business is not one specific major but a multidisciplinary major or a dual major with an international orientation. Examples include area studies such as European studies or Asian studies and dual majors in business and foreign languages, economics and international studies/political science, or any technical major (engineering, chemistry, or biology) with some other major that is international in focus. To most internationally oriented companies, multidisciplinary degrees are considered better preparation and more desirable for international business careers than a degree in any single subject. They are also typically considered better preparation by most graduate programs in international business you may subsequently attempt to enter.

An increasing number of colleges and universities are now offering undergraduate degree programs in international business or multidisciplinary programs in business and foreign language or international studies. Several of these programs are described briefly later in this chapter.

It is also desirable to take several courses in business at the undergraduate level, regardless of your major. The basic courses in business, such as accounting, marketing, finance, and management, will provide you with some understanding of business in general and which kind of job in business you are most interested in and suited for. In addition, many business schools offer special sections of these courses to nonbusiness majors. If your degree's requirements permit you to take only one business course, a course in business for nonbusiness majors is probably the best one to take. If not available, the first course in management is a good alternative because it typically provides a general overview of business.

Finally, it is important that you recognize that there still are not many entry-level jobs in international business, and there are even fewer for people with only undergraduate degrees. Most entry jobs in international business for persons with undergraduate degrees initially involve export or import documentation, language translation, international shipping, or tourism. Or they may be slightly higher-level jobs in smaller companies involved in, or planning to become involved in, international trade. Excellent preparation for these kind of entry-level jobs is a degree that combines international business and some other international field, such as foreign languages or international studies.

Master's Level Education

At the master's-degree level, there are many opportunities to further broaden and deepen your international education. More importantly, there are new opportunities to deepen your knowledge in a specific area of international business and to develop many of the highly specialized skills needed for a career in international business.

Regardless of what subject you majored in as an undergraduate, most companies will want you to have a master's degree in business. This does not mean that companies will not hire you if you have a nonbusiness graduate degree, but your choices of companies and occupations will be more limited. Several notable exceptions include graduate degrees in law and in technical and scientific fields such as information systems, chemistry, physics, biology, and engineering. Even in these cases, however, your initial and subsequent opportunities for a career in international business will be influenced by the number and types of international courses you take in addition to whatever degree you obtain. For example, someone with an engineering degree plus foreign language skills or international business courses will have a competitive advantage over someone with only an engineering degree.

In terms of a business degree, the first thing to consider is the type of business degree. Several major options include a master of business administration (MBA), master's degrees in specific functional areas of business (such as a master of taxation or a master of personnel and employee relations), and specialized master's degrees in international business.

The most widely available and internationally recognized business degree is the MBA. Most MBA degree programs require two years to complete, and many of them require several years of business experience prior to enrolling. The vast majority of MBA programs require courses in all major functional areas of business and provide opportunities for concentration (specialization) in one of these functional areas, such as finance, marketing, or management. However, some universities still do not offer courses in international business. Most do not offer a major (concentration) in international business or even require that a single international business course be taken. And even fewer business schools require students to learn a foreign language or undertake a study or work experience in a foreign country.

While this suggests that international business educational opportunities are rather limited in MBA programs, it is somewhat misleading. Many MBA programs have an internationalized curriculum even if they do not have specific courses or concentrations in international business. In an internationalized curriculum, the international aspects of business are integrated with regular MBA courses. For example, the international aspects of finance are covered in the basic MBA course on corporate finance. The majority of MBA programs that have international content in their curriculum have opted for this internationalized course approach rather than having international courses or majors. In addition, many MBA programs offer semester-abroad options for students who wish to pursue them.

The preceding comments pertaining to MBA programs apply equally to master's-degree programs in specialized functional areas of business. Only a small percentage offer or require an international business course. But unlike many MBA programs, almost none offer semester-abroad options or a concentration in the international aspects of the specialized functional area. As a result, these programs are not particularly well suited for people seeking a career in international business.

Given that you can emphasize international business in many MBA programs, a more difficult choice is whether to obtain an MBA degree or to obtain a specialized degree in international business. The latter are not always considered MBAs and typically have *international* in the name of the degree, such as a master of international business studies, master of international business, or master of international management. These specialized master's-degree programs in international business almost always have foreign language and international studies requirements and also require a whole series of international business courses beyond the kinds of courses required in a typical MBA program. Most of these degree programs also have study-abroad or overseas internship options, and a few of them require that some kind of international experience be obtained before graduation. Several of the leading specialized international business degree programs are described in greater detail later in this chapter.

The choice between these specialized international business programs and MBA programs with international content involves several considerations. First, the MBA is a more recognized degree throughout the world and needs little explanation to a potential employer. Specialized international business degrees are newer, not as well known, and require greater explanation. Second, generally, universities offering the most prestigious MBA degrees do not offer specialized international business degrees. Therefore, if you want a master's degree in business from one of the highest prestige schools, such as Harvard, Chicago, or Stanford, you do not have the option of obtaining a specialized international business degree. Third, most MBA programs provide more concentration in a specific functional area of business, and most potential employers like specialization in a functional area. Thus, if you pursue a specialized international business degree, you may have to trade off specialization in a functional area for a specialization in international business, and many firms still prefer the former to the latter. Fourth, there are more jobs available initially and subsequently in purely functional areas compared to the international activities of these functional areas and to international business in general. Therefore, the number of jobs from which to pick is often greater for MBAs. Finally, schools that offer an MBA vastly outnumber those that offer a specialized international business degree. As a result, it is easier to gain admittance to the former than to the latter.

Most of these observations may appear to support getting an MBA rather than a specialized international business degree. So why seek a specialized degree in international business instead of an MBA? There are several reasons. First, there is a steadily increasing demand for people with considerable education and specialized training in international business. MBAs typically do not have this degree of education and training. Second, while there are fewer entry-level jobs in international business, the mid-level and senior-level positions in international business are most likely to be given to people with the greatest amount of international education and training. So while MBAs may have more advantages initially in getting a job, people with specialized degrees in international business have the advantage subsequently for international jobs. Third, even if you do not obtain an international business job initially or subsequently, you will probably be better prepared to perform your job because virtually all jobs and companies are affected by international trends and events. Finally, your educational experience and subsequent outlook on life will be broader and richer from having obtained a specialized degree in international business.

Doctoral Level Education

A doctoral degree in international business is primarily a degree for people who seek an academic career in international business or, in some cases, a research, consulting, or government career in international business. For the most part, a doctoral degree in business or international business is of little value for a practitioner career in international business. Businesses generally prefer employees with more pragmatic education and training (compared to theoretical) and would rather you had gained several more years of business experience than having spent those years in a Ph.D. program. So if it is a practitioner career you are really interested in, it is advisable to stop your formal education at the master's-degree level and get down to, and into, business. If an academic or research career in international business is what you seek, read on.

Most, if not all, of the considerations concerning choosing a master's degree apply equally to choosing a doctoral degree. Most business schools strongly prefer a Ph.D. in business (compared to other disciplines), far fewer universities offer a doctoral degree in international business, fewer academic positions are available in international business, and most universities prefer faculty with greater specialization in a functional area than in international business. Ph.D. programs in international business may also take longer to complete because of foreign language or international studies requirements not found in most Ph.D. programs in business.

Most of the same reasons for obtaining a specialized master's degree in international business apply to obtaining a doctoral degree in international business. With demand increasing so rapidly for people to teach others about international business, the demand for international business faculty is increasing faster than the supply of faculty appropriately trained. To many people, a Ph.D. in international business is a more interesting and enriching educational experience than a Ph.D. in a domestic or functional area. Teaching international business courses and conducting international business research are also more interesting and enriching than teaching and doing research in a purely domestic context. There are more opportunities for international travel and for interaction with people from other cultures. In addition, more and more of the most important public policy issues facing countries will be related to international business. As a result, Ph.D.s in international business will have an increasingly important role to play in these policy issue deliberations and their resolution.

So in business and in academia, those who like complex intellectual challenges, diversity of experiences, and an enriched life should pursue specialized training in international business. The following section describes the most innovative and comprehensive specialized degree programs available in the formal education system in the United States in the 1990s.

UNDERGRADUATE SPECIALIZED DEGREE PROGRAMS

Specialized international business degree programs at the undergraduate level are a fairly recent development and are few, but growing, in number. One of the most comprehensive programs is offered by Eastern Michigan University (EMU) in Ypsilanti, Michigan. Because it is the largest program and the one several other universities have modeled their programs after, EMU's program deserves special mention. Other universities that offer smaller programs are also described briefly.

Eastern Michigan University

Established in 1979, EMU's bachelor of arts in language and international trade degree is a truly interdisciplinary program requiring all students to take courses in business, foreign languages, and international studies. In the foreign language area, a minimum of 18 semester hours is required in a specific foreign language at the upper division level, including three business language courses. Students who enter the program with no previous foreign language training may have to take as many as 16 additional credit hours of foreign language. Foreign language specializations include French, German, Japanese, and Spanish. Students must also take nine credit hours of courses in the international studies area, such as internationally focused courses in geography, history, and political science. In addition, students are required to take 30 credit hours in business and economics and complete a cooperative education program in international business. The co-op program requires each student to work full-time for four months in an administrative setting either inside or outside the United States. To arrange these practical training experiences, EMU established an International Cooperative Educational Exchange Consortium that works with universities outside the United States on a co-op exchange basis. EMU's bachelor of arts in language and international trade program has more than 150 students enrolled annually.

In 1987, EMU initiated a joint degree program called the BBA/BA in language and world business. This joint degree program takes 5 1/2 years to complete and includes all the requirements of EMU's BA in language and international trade degree plus the additional course requirements for a BBA in international business. As a result, students in the joint degree program take much more course work in the business area than those who are in the bachelor of arts program. Due to the additional year required to obtain the joint degree, only about 90 students are enrolled in the program.

Other Universities

In a format very similar to the BA program at EMU, a bachelor of arts degree in language and international trade was established in 1987 at Clemson University in Clemson, South Carolina. The main differences in Clemson's program are that slightly more language and international studies courses are required, and students must select a professional option from one of four offered: marketing, international textile marketing, international forest products marketing, or international tourism. More than 140 students enrolled in Clemson's program the first year it was offered, and 185 entered in 1993.

Other universities that offer similarly configured, specialized programs at the undergraduate level include Southern Illinois University, Auburn University, and San Diego State University.

SPECIALIZED MASTER'S DEGREE PROGRAMS

There are several well-established specialized international business degree programs at the graduate level especially worthy of mention because they require all students to combine business course work with foreign language training and international studies courses. Among the oldest and best-known ones are the Master of International Management at the American Graduate School of International Management (AGSIM) in Glendale, Arizona; the MBA in international management at the Monterey Institute of International Studies in Monterey, California; the Lauder Institute program at the University of Pennsylvania in Philadelphia, Pennsylvania; and the Master of International Business Studies (MIBS) program at the University of South Carolina in Columbia, South Carolina.

Of these programs, the two that deserve the most special recognition are the ones at the University of South Carolina and the University of Pennsylvania. Their special recognition stems from the fact that both programs require overseas language and cultural training and a corporate internship abroad as part of their degree requirements. A recently established International Management Fellows (IMF) program at UCLA also fits into this special category as do other relatively new programs at the University of Miami and Memphis State University.

AGSIM

The oldest and largest specialized degree program in international business, AGSIM's Master of International Management degree, was the first to require all students to combine business course work with language training and courses in international studies. Established in the late 1940s, the program offered by AGSIM (then and occasionally even now known as Thunderbird) is normally a 15-month, minimum of 42-semester-hour program with roughly 50 percent in business, 25 percent in foreign language, and 25 percent in international studies.

Fifteen hundred students attend AGSIM each year, and there are more than 27,000 AGSIM alumni, often referred to as T-Birds. Foreign language specializations include Arabic, Chinese, French, German, Italian, Japanese, Portuguese, Russian, Spanish, and English as a second language. AGSIM also offers semester-length study-abroad experiences in several countries, such as Norway, Germany, China, Japan, France, Mexico, and Spain. However, neither study-abroad nor overseas internship experiences are required as part of AGSIM's degree program.

Perhaps the most unique aspect of AGSIM is that it is a single-degree institution. As a result, all students attending AGSIM receive the only degree offered, and all faculty at AGSIM teach only in the Master of International Management Program.

The Monterey Institute

The language training and international studies programs at the Monterey Institute had been in existence for nearly 20 years before its MBA in International Management degree was established in 1976. It is a 64-semester-hour program that can be completed normally in two years and has a curriculum mix of 70 percent business, 20 percent foreign language, and 10 percent international studies. Monterey's degree program is much smaller in terms of enrollment than AGSIM's program, having about 200 students enrolled (first- and second-year students combined). Like AGSIM's program, the Monterey Institute's program encourages but does not require any overseas study or internship program. Language specializations offered at Monterey include Arabic, Chinese, French, German, Italian, Japanese, Korean, Portuguese, Russian, Spanish, and English as a second language. Eighty-four students entered in 1993.

The University of Pennsylvania

Inaugurated in 1984, a special degree program offered through the University of Pennsylvania's Lauder Institute is one of the most comprehensive in the United States. It is actually a dual degree program, resulting in an MBA degree from the Wharton School of Business and a masters' degree in international studies from the School of Arts and Sciences. It is an intensive 24-month, 72-credit-hour program with a curriculum that is approximately 60 percent business, 20 percent foreign language, and 20 percent international studies. Foreign languages offered include Chinese, French, German, Japanese, Portuguese, Russian, Spanish, and English as a second language.

There are several characteristics that particularly distinguish Pennsylvania's specialized degree program from those at AGSIM and Monterey. One is the requirement that all students must already have a high level of proficiency in a foreign language before beginning the program. A second difference is that all students are required during the first summer to participate in an eight-week foreign language and culture training program taught outside the United States in countries such as Brazil, China, France, Germany, India, Venezuela, and Russia. A third difference is that all U.S. students are required to complete a three-month internship abroad during the second summer of the program.

The program's high admission standards and tuition resulted in an incoming class of only 53 students in 1993.

The University of South Carolina

Established in 1974, the University of South Carolina's Master of International Business Studies (MIBS) degree was the first program to require overseas language and cultural training and an overseas corporate internship for all of its U.S. students in addition to required courses in business and international studies. (The MIBS program's non-U.S. students follow a similar curriculum but intern in the United States, improve their English language skills, and study the economic geography and political system of the United States.) The basic, 24-month

MIBS curriculum is approximately 60 percent business, 30 percent foreign language, and 10 percent international studies. Exceptions are the lengthier language and cultural specializations in Arabic, Chinese, Japanese, and Korean for which the curriculum mix is roughly 40 percent business, 40 percent language, and 20 percent international studies.

The MIBS program's language specializations in French, German, Italian, Portuguese, Spanish, Russian, and English as a second language are generally 24-month, 72-credit-hour programs. The MIBS program's Arabic, Chinese, Japanese, and Korean language specializations are normally 36-month-long programs, at least half of which takes place in Egypt, Japan, Taiwan, China, or Korea. The additional 12 months of study are due to the much greater difficulty of these three languages and are necessary because the MIBS program (unlike the program at the University of Pennsylvania) does not require any foreign language proficiency prior to enrollment.

There are nearly 1,500 MIBS alumni working in over 50 different countries, 75 percent of whom have international business responsibilities as the major portion of their jobs. Most MIBS alumni work for the world's largest multinational firms in their home countries or abroad.

The most distinguishing feature of the MIBS program is that it is the only program that requires a six-month corporate internship in a foreign setting. Another key difference is that with over 350 students enrolled annually, MIBS is the largest graduate-degree program in international business at a college or school of business accredited by the American Assembly of Collegiate Schools of Business (AACSB). A third distinguishing feature is cost. The University of South Carolina is a state-supported university, resulting in significantly lower tuition compared to the tuition at private colleges and universities. In cooperation with the Business and Economics University of Vienna (Wirtschaftsuniversitat Wien), the University of South Carolina also offers a 15-month International MBA entirely in English, the first half of which takes place in Vienna, followed by advanced course work and a field consultancy project in South Carolina. Between 30 and 40 students from different countries are enrolled annually in the program.

Honorable Mentions

Also worthy of mention are several comparatively newer programs at UCLA, Memphis State, and the University of Miami (Florida) as well as one alternative education program offered by the Management Education Institute of the international consulting firm of Arthur D. Little. Memphis State's International MBA (IMBA) program began in 1993 and was modeled after South Carolina's MIBS program. The major difference in program structure is that the overseas experience aspect of Memphis State's program lasts only one semester and can consist of studying at a foreign university rather than a corporate internship. Twenty-one students were admitted in 1993, choosing among the language specializations of French, German, and Spanish,

The University of Miami's new program (launched in 1992) is advertised as an MIBS program, but actually results in the conferring of two separate degrees: an MBA and an MS in International Business Studies. It too was based largely on USC's MIBS program but requires only a semester (4 months) of overseas experience (normally a corporate internship). In 1993, language options included French, German, and Spanish and approximately 100 students entered the program.

The International Management Fellows (IMF) program at UCLA represents another approach to international business education. Students follow the normal MBA curriculum at UCLA's Anderson Graduate School of Management plus complete additional requirements that result in the conferring of an IMF certificate in addition to the MBA degree. The requirements for the International Management Fellow program include course work inside and outside the United States to enhance students' existing foreign language proficiency and a six-month period abroad that is normally split between academic studies and a corporate internship. Language options are French, German, Japanese, and Spanish for the 23 students who began the IMF program in 1993.

Finally, the Arthur D. Little Management Education Institute in Cambridge, Massachusetts, offers an 11-month Master of Science in Management with an international business concentration that is distinctly different from all the others mentioned above. Its major distinctions are its brevity, faculty, and student body. Roughly 95 percent of the students are from countries other than the United States, perhaps constituting the most international student group in a general admission U.S. academic degree program. Of the program's faculty, roughly 60 percent are practicing members of A.D. Little's consulting firm, giving the program a very applied focus. (The remainder of the instruction is done by faculty employed at nearby academic institutions.) About 55 students attend each year.

DOCTORAL PROGRAMS IN INTERNATIONAL BUSINESS

Most doctoral programs in business do not offer a specialization in international business. Few offer a degree that has *international business* in the official name of the degree—including many that do offer an international business specialization, major, or concentration. However, there are many significant differences among doctoral programs in international business in terms of the comprehensiveness of the international components in their curricula.

The more comprehensive programs require all international majors to have or develop a proficiency in at least one foreign language and to take at least four courses in some aspect of international business. Several well-established and highly regarded programs that have one or both of these features include the University of Michigan, New York University, Columbia University, Indiana University, the University of Washington (Seattle), and UCLA.

The most comprehensive type of program additionally requires an overseas experience of some kind, such as a study-abroad component or an overseas teaching, research, consulting, or internship experience. As of 1993, only one doctoral level business program in the United States required this overseas experiential component: the University of South Carolina. At the University of South Carolina, doctoral students majoring in international business must first meet all the normal degree requirements that other doctoral students must meet. In addition, they must take at least five courses in international business (two of which must be courses in international business theory and international business research methods), pass a proficiency exam in a foreign language of their choice, and spend several months outside the United States teaching, studying, doing research, or working for a firm or some other kind of organization. Currently, no other doctoral program in business requires such a comprehensive international component.

Degree Programs Offered Outside the United States

Another option worth considering is obtaining a business degree in a foreign country. After all, studying business in a foreign country provides an excellent opportunity to learn about and actually experience a foreign culture while getting a business degree in the process. Many business schools throughout the world offer degree programs and curricula similar to those offered in the United States, taught by faculty equally qualified as those in the United States. The major obstacle for most U.S. students is being sufficiently fluent in a foreign language to undertake a degree program abroad. However, even though the vast majority of business schools abroad utilize the local language in their classes, a growing number now offer courses and even full degree programs in English. One example is the Helsinki School of Economics and Business in Finland, which offers an English language International MBA program. But even then, a little Finnish is helpful in terms of living in Helsinki. So if English is your native and only language, you might feel more comfortable in another English environment, such as the United Kingdom, Australia, New Zealand, the British West Indies (and other former British territories in the Caribbean), or the English-speaking provinces of Canada.

Leaving aside the issue of language, virtually every country has at least one institution of higher learning that is particularly well known for business programs. Examples include INSEAD in France, the London Business School in England, the IMD in Switzerland, the Business and Economic University of Vienna in Austria, the Helsinki School of Economics and Business in Finland, IESA and ESADE in Spain, University of the Andes in Columbia, the Gertulio Vargas Institute in Brazil, Keio and Waseda universities in Japan, Seoul National and Yonsei universities in Korea, the University of International

Business and Economics in China, the University of Chile, INCAE in Nicaragua and Costa Rica, the Monterey Institute of Technology in Mexico, and the University of Western Ontario, McGill, and the University of British Columbia in Canada.

While all of these universities offer excellent degrees in business, the content and quality of their degrees may be less known or recognized in other countries, including your own. As a result, potential employers in your country may not be able to assess them as easily as they could degrees from local institutions they know better. However, multinational companies do see advantages to hiring people who have been educated abroad, particularly when the education took place in the country where the corporate headquarters is located or where they have major operations. For example, U.S. multinational firms like to hire non-U.S. citizens who have been educated in U.S. business schools to work for the company in the students' home countries. Similarly, European multinationals see advantages in hiring personnel who have been educated in several different European countries or in Europe and some other regions of the world. A student's international educational background suggest to multinational enterprises that the potential employee has demonstrated initiative, flexibility, cultural adaptability, and a certain degree of risk taking that are considered desirable attributes of future executives. So if you can handle the language and cultural adaptation aspects of studying abroad, it may prove worth it. If nothing else, it will be an enlightening and enriching life experience that you will never forget.

CONTINUING EDUCATION PROGRAMS

Continuing education programs continue the education begun in the formal educational process. They are offered virtually everywhere by a wide range of organizations, including colleges and universities, companies, government agencies, and many types of private organizations. Their most distinguishing characteristics are their shortness in length (typically one day to two weeks) and their focus on highly specific topics.

Some continuing education programs are skill-building in nature, others are highly job related, and still others seek to increase participants' general awareness or understanding of a particular subject. Some specific categories of continuing education are seminars, conferences, and short courses (typically of a not-for-credit variety). These programs are usually oriented to either practitioners or academics but are occasionally offered to both groups simultaneously. Yet regardless of the participants, the best programs have both academics and practitioners as speakers because each has some unique perspectives and skills that the other does not have.

Many continuing education programs provide excellent opportunities to prepare you for a career in international business or to help you develop more advanced skills in international business. Examples of the first are programs about the basic aspects and functions of international business and programs about various regions or countries of the world. Examples of the second are programs about advanced techniques in international negotiating or foreign exchange risk management.

Another important benefit from participating in continuing education programs is the interaction you have with others who are interested in the topic. Many of them are probably facing the same problems or challenges you and your organization are facing. Important future contacts can be established in this interaction process, and you can also learn from the experiences and perspectives of other participants as well as those of the speakers. Also of importance is the fact that continuing education often offers the first opportunity for many people to learn about international business. Some people did not have or take the opportunity to learn about international business during their formal education period. In addition, many people who did study international business in school have not kept up-to-date on current developments and techniques or have forgotten most, if not all, of what they learned previously.

For all of these reasons, continuing education is a valuable method for preparing for international business careers and for advancing in them. The more you participate in continuing education of an international variety, the more qualified you will become.

ON-THE-JOB TRAINING

Many people currently in international business jobs had little or no educational preparation in international business. They learned about international business by doing it. In other words, they learned international business on the job. In most of these cases, they were already working in a domestic capacity when their firm first became involved in international business. Typically, their existing technical skills and experience with the company, coupled with the fact that no one else in the company had any international training, resulted in their being selected to handle the new international activity. By trial and error they learned the international complexities of doing their formerly domestic job.

For example, an unsolicited order for a company's product was made by a company in another country. The sales department had never exported any product, the shipping department had never shipped any product abroad, and the finance department had never extended credit to a foreign buyer or had to deal with foreign currencies. But because the company wanted to make the sale, all of the appropriate departments had to learn enough about international business to make the sale successful. Each subsequent time the company made an export sale, its personnel learned more about international business and began to develop more advanced international business skills. Over time, more of the company's personnel became involved and skilled in international business, and the on-the-job learning process continued.

This process and pattern of learning international business on the job still continues today even though there are more people with prior, formal education in international business. One reason is that there is more international business being conducted than there are people with international business backgrounds. Another reason is that having studied international business is not the same as being able to do international business. Many aspects of doing international business can be learned only through experience. It is through doing international business that you more fully learn and understand it. Finally, gaining international experience is the way you prepare yourself for higher level jobs in international business and ultimately for the top management jobs that have global responsibilities.

For all of these reasons, learning international business on the job is a necessary and valuable part of an international business career. And the more opportunities you have to gain such experiences, the better. But while there may be no substitute for firsthand experience, it is better to be as prepared as possible before you have to experience international business. Therefore, get as well prepared as you possibly can.

BECOMING AND STAYING INFORMED BY OTHER METHODS

The formal education system, the continuing education system, and on-the-job training provide structured, formal ways of becoming and staying informed and of developing specific international skills. However, they are by no means the only ways. A great deal of learning takes place in an unstructured, informal manner. Some very common ways are reading books, magazines, and newspapers and watching television news programs, educational television, and even travelogues. Other ways are by interacting with people more knowledgeable than you are and by observing people and their activities.

In terms of international business, there are many good printed sources of information you can and should read. For general information, there are many college textbooks about international business, international marketing, international finance, and the other functional fields within international business. These textbooks can be purchased from university bookstores and, in some cases, from other kinds of bookstores. Practitioner-oriented books on international business topics as well as books about specific countries and cultures are available in most major bookstores. One particularly entertaining and enlightening book about international business is *Big Business Blunders,* written by David Ricks and published by Dow Jones-Irwin in 1983. This book contains examples of over 200 actual business blunders made by companies in their international activities because they did not sufficiently understand and prepare for doing business in a foreign setting.

Magazines and newspapers provide more current information about international business trends and activities. In terms of magazines, *The*

Economist (published in England) is one of the best and most comprehensive and also provides a non-U.S. perspective about what is happening in the world. London's *Financial Times* does an equally good job in the newspaper category. Major business magazines such as *Business Week, Fortune,* and *Forbes* are excellent U.S. sources of information about international business. In the U.S. newspaper category, excellent sources are the *Wall Street Journal,* the *Journal of Commerce,* and the *New York Times.* There are also many business magazines published in other countries that are also good sources of information about international business such as *L'Expansion* in France, *Wirtschaftswoche* in Germany, *El Mondo* in Italy, and *President* in Japan. However, these magazines are published in the language of their country, so you must be able to read their languages.

Personally interacting with people who teach or conduct international business is still another way of becoming and staying informed about international business. Seek them out and talk to them about what is happening in international business. Some good places to meet international business practitioners are international trade organizations or clubs; they are generally open to anyone who is interested in joining. Attending internationally oriented continuing education programs is another good way of meeting international business practitioners. International business academics are most easily found in colleges of business, although not all colleges of business have them. Finally, just interacting with people who have international interests and experiences can be useful, even if international business is not their specialty. You can learn a lot about foreign countries and cultures in this manner—information that can be useful to you subsequently in an international business career.

There are many different ways of preparing for a career in international business and for staying informed. You should pursue as many of them as possible to gain true expertise. If you are still in the formal education system, take as many international courses as you can and, if feasible, pursue an overseas academic or internship experience while you are still in school. If you are already out of the formal education system, become as active as you can in internationally oriented continuing education programs and organizations. And no matter what your status is, read whatever you can in newspapers and magazines about international events and trends, have as much personal interaction as possible with foreigners and internationally oriented people in your community, and, money and time permitting, do some international traveling. The more you learn, the better prepared and informed you will be.

CHAPTER 7

CHARTING YOUR CAREER IN INTERNATIONAL BUSINESS

The preceding chapters of this book have described what international business is, its evolution and prospects for the future, its specialized fields, and various ways of preparing for careers. With this informational background, you should now have a better idea of whether a career in international business seems right for you. Of course you will not really know if it is right for you until you have actually experienced it. And to be able to experience it, you first have to get a job.

This final chapter discusses initially getting a job, advancing in your chosen career, and options later in your career you may wish to consider. Because these activities and options are different for practitioners and academics, the first part of the chapter is most relevant for people seeking primarily a practitioner career and the second part for those seeking primarily an academic career. The word *primarily* is used because these two major career options are not mutually exclusive. Many academicians gain business experience before pursuing an academic career and have options for a business career both during and after their academic career. Similarly, many practitioners pursue academic careers after retiring from business or do some teaching while they are still in business. People who have specialized in international business are not exceptions to these career-mixing options.

PRACTITIONER CAREERS

Getting a Job

To get your initial job, you must first become aware of jobs that are available. Second, you must get in contact with the appropriate person who influences the hiring process. Third, you must be sufficiently persuasive to obtain a formal interview. In most cases you will have to do well enough in the first interview to be given follow-up interviews. And in some cases you may have to take and pass certain examinations or other types of aptitude or skill proficiency tests before, during, or even after the interview process. In virtually all cases you will be asked to provide references. Finally, it may be necessary to apply for a job and be interviewed by a firm that represents the company where the job will be.

BECOMING AWARE OF OPPORTUNITIES

One of the best and most prevalent sources of information about available jobs is classified advertisements in newspapers (and occasionally magazines), especially business-oriented ones. These advertisements typically provide information about job responsibilities and requirements, qualifications needed, location, and, many times, salary and benefits. They also contain the name, position, and address of the appropriate person to contact. While some newspapers and magazines have nationwide coverage of jobs available (such as the *Wall Street Journal,* the *Journal of Commerce* or *USA Today*), most have regional or local coverage. Therefore, if you are looking for a job in a certain region or city, you should also obtain copies of newspapers and magazines that serve that area or city.

Another good source for leads is a placement center at a college or university. Companies that recruit there either in person or by posting an announcement typically provide the same kinds of information contained in classified advertisements. If you are a student or an alumnus, use the university's placement service to the greatest extent possible. If you are neither a student nor alumnus, it is still advisable, if permitted, to examine the placement bulletin boards or other material in the placement center that contains information about available jobs. Befriending the director and staff of the placement center is also a wise strategy, regardless of your status. They may know of other opportunities and people to contact that may be appropriate for you if they know you, like you, and think you may be qualified.

Another source of job leads is job placement/recruiting companies. Their role is to find suitable employees for their client companies and to find suitable jobs for the individuals who use their placement services. However, these types of companies are usually fee based, requiring that the individual they place or the company they recruit for pay them a fee. In addition, you cannot expect them to assist you unless you become one of their clients.

Another source of information is the companies in which you seek employment. By directly contacting their personnel office, you can learn what kinds of jobs are available and other job-related information. You can also contact someone in the firm whom you already know to obtain this kind of information or learn from him or her who is the best person to contact for this information other than those who work in personnel. Even if no jobs suitable for you exist in their company, any of these people may know of job openings in other companies.

No low-cost means of obtaining information about job openings should be ignored. You never know ahead of time where the best leads can be obtained.

CONTACTING COMPANIES

Companies hire throughout the year, so contacting them at any time can be successful. However, hiring entry-level personnel typically coincides with university graduation. As a result, recruiting activities for these positions are more concentrated during the fall and spring semesters. It is also during these periods that the largest percentage of on-campus recruiting is conducted. So if you are still in school, be sure to be in contact with your school's placement service and follow all of its procedures for being eligible for on-campus interviews. Using your university's placement service is an excellent way for you to be put in contact with potential employers without having to contact them yourself.

To properly contact companies, you will need to have a resume highlighting your background, qualifications, and interests. There are several different approaches and theories about effective resume form and content. The conventional approach is to limit the resume to one page, follow a well-established and fairly standard format, and use white paper and black, conventional typeface. The nonconventional approach is not to follow the conventional approach. Due to the conservative and traditional nature of most large companies, a conventional resume is likely to be received better than a nonconventional one.

Regardless of the approach you take, a good resume begins with a statement of your specific career goals and objectives, both short term and long term. Because you will be applying for a job in business, the resume should emphasize your business-related qualifications such as work experience, business courses taken, and, if applicable, any business degree received. Your resume should also highlight any of your major accomplishments of potential relevance to business firms such as leadership activities, honors received, and anything else that indicates superior performance on your part.

Since international business is your ultimate, if not immediate, goal, your resume should also emphasize your international background and abilities, such as international courses, foreign language skills, and previous international travel and living experiences. However, because of the limited number of entry-level jobs in international business, be careful about stressing too heavily your international interests and qualifications. You have only a limited amount of space on a resume, and most firms will be looking for qualifications that they can use immediately. Therefore, your resume should emphasize your noninternational aspects as much, if not more than, your international aspects. Finally, form is as important as content. A well-organized, neatly prepared, and succinct resume makes a very favorable impression on those who receive it.

In addition to having a good resume, it is equally important to develop a good cover letter to accompany your resume. The cover letter should quickly and succinctly identify the match between your interests and qualifications and the job position for which you are applying. If at all possible, it should be addressed to a specific person in the company rather than to a job title such as *director of personnel.* Addressing it to a specific person shows that you have done your homework properly and also conveys the impression that you are targeting the firm rather than doing a mass mail-out. In preparing both your resume and cover letter, it is advisable to get some advice from career counseling professionals and spend the extra money required to have them prepared and printed professionally. There are many helpful books on resume and cover letter preparation, including *How to Write a Winning Resume* by Deborah Perlmutter Bloch and *Cover Letters They Don't Forget* by Eric Martin and Karyn Langhorne. Purchase them from a bookstore or check them out of your local library.

Another issue in contacting companies is whether to use a shotgun or rifle approach. The shotgun approach is to mail your resume and cover letter to as many firms as possible, using a very standardized resume and cover letter. The rifle approach is to select a much smaller number of firms to contact and to tailor your resume and cover letter to each specific firm. For jobs in international business, the rifle approach is more likely to be successful because fewer firms will have a need for someone with your international qualifications, and the types of international opportunities each firm offers will vary considerably. To identify the most likely firms, look at annual reports for information about their international activities and consult various directories that contain information about firms and their international activities.

In contacting companies, it often pays to be creative and thorough in your approach by sending your resume to people in several different divisions, functional areas, and geographic locations of the same company. Some companies practice very decentralized hiring, and sending just one resume to one person may not be effective as a result. In addition, one person is not likely to be aware of all the positions available throughout the company or might not be able to assess properly your unique qualifications.

Regardless of the approach you take, you should be prepared for outright rejection, exemplified by the dreaded form rejection letter. You must also be prepared for a more carefully considered rejection because, even though you may be qualified, you are not as qualified as others who applied. In any event, you need to be persistent in your efforts in contacting companies and not become easily discouraged. Competition for good jobs is always tough. Finally, it is generally unwise to simply drop in unannounced (without having made an appointment).

As an alternative to directly contacting companies yourself, you might also consider using placement firms who do this service for you. Before doing so, however, it is wise to investigate their placement record, the types of jobs and companies they place people in, their geographic coverage, and their fee system.

INTERVIEWING

The interviewing process is the next formal step in getting a job and, for most companies, the most important. It is also generally the most tense and nerve-racking step for job applicants. No matter how qualified you appear on your resume, companies want to evaluate your physical appearance; verbal communication abilities; and general emotional, psychological, and attitudinal outlook. These evaluations can best be done in an interview format, be it in a formal or informal setting.

While you may question the importance of physical appearance and grooming, companies consider them important. As an employee of a company, you represent the image the company wants to project. For example, some companies, such as accounting firms, banks, and other financial institutions, prefer a conservative image. By looking at companies' annual reports and other public relations publications, you can get a general sense of the image they are trying to project. Placement counselors can also provide this type of corporate image information. In addition, some job positions/specializations within a company have images that call for a certain type of appearance. For example, positions that deal with money generally have a more conservative image than those that deal with consumer marketing and advertising. As a result, it is important to dress appropriately for the company and the type of job you are considering. And regardless of how you dress, it is equally important to be well groomed. A sloppy appearance suggests to an interviewer that you are a sloppy thinker, do not know any better, are not taking the interview seriously, are not suitable for a business career, or some combination of the above.

It is extremely important that you adequately research the company and its industry before the interview. The greater knowledge you have about the company's history, current operations, key management philosophies, personnel, and what is happening in the company's industry, the more intelligent questions you can ask during the interview and the more you can impress the interviewer. It is also important to have a good understanding of the general responsibilities of the position for which you are applying. For example, if you really do not know what a financial planner does but are applying for a job as a financial planner, you are not likely to favorably impress the interviewer.

Another important and advisable preparation for an interview is to take a class or attend a seminar about interviewing techniques and the interviewing process (or meet with placement counselors who can provide you with this type of information). Experienced placement professionals can give you important interviewing tips and advice and, in some cases, conduct practice interviews with you and then analyze them to determine how you can improve your performance. With each actual interview you should gain insights on how to improve your performance, but some people never fully understand their interviewing weaknesses. As a result, they fail to get the jobs they seek even though they may be qualified. *How to Have a Winning Job Interview* by Deborah Perlmutter Bloch is an excellent guide to the interview process that outlines all the steps you need to take in preparing for an interview.

First interviews are generally short. As a result, you have very little time to make a good and lasting impression. During the interview itself, be prepared to answer questions about your background, qualifications, accomplishments, and career interests and goals. Also be prepared to answer why you are interested in the specific job and company. In responding to such questions, be brief, specific, and thoughtful in your answers. In addition, be prepared to ask equally brief, specific, and thoughtful questions of the interviewer about the job itself, general working conditions in the company, training and career development programs offered, and career advancement policies and procedures. Throughout the interview, be candid, personable, respectful, confident, and enthusiastic and avoid being boastful, arrogant, too wordy, or too humble. Maintain good eye contact with the interviewer and be observant of the interviewer's body language in addition to what he or she is saying. And because there are not many entry-level jobs in international business, it is also important for you to emphasize that, even though you are interested ultimately in a career involving international business, you are most interested in getting your business career started. If you insist on a job immediately in international business, you will have far fewer job offers from which to select and may pass up a good employment opportunity that could lead ultimately to one with international responsibilities.

In most cases, a second and possibly a third interview will be required before a final decision will be made by the company. But in order to be invited back for a subsequent interview, you must do well on the first interview. Hence the importance of making a good first impression. It is during the later interviews that it is more appropriate to ask questions about salary, fringe benefit packages, moving expenses, and other financial terms of employment. Asking these kinds of questions during the first interview is often considered bad interviewing form. The interviewers know you are interested in this kind of information and will be happy to provide it later once they have decided you are a strong contender for the position.

At the conclusion of each interview, thank the interviewer for taking time to talk with you, and if you are still interested in the job, say so. Immediately after leaving the interview, take a few minutes to write a brief summary of what was discussed during the interview, your general impressions of the interview, and any important questions that remain to be discussed. You will be surprised how useful these summaries will be, particularly after you have interviewed with several companies or several times with the same company. Within a day or two after the interview, send a formal thank-you letter to the interviewer. Good manners are always appreciated and considered indicative of maturity. Follow-up letters also keep your name in the minds of the interviewers.

There may be times when you encounter a situation where you do not know the name of the company that is offering the position. This situation is most likely to occur if you are being initially interviewed by a professional recruiting company, but it can also result from an advertisement that does not specify the name of the company with the available position. What you are likely to be given is some clues about the company's identity, for example, "a medium size, diversified consumer products company based in the Midwest . . ." In such cases, it is more difficult to prepare for an interview and tailor your approach. However, you should not automatically reject this kind of blind opportunity if the position available appears to match your interests and qualifications.

Finally, keep in mind that interviewing is a two-way process. The company wants and needs a great deal of information about you, and you about it. While all interviews are conducted largely on the company's terms, you have some control over the information exchange process. It is necessary that you obtain complete answers to the questions most important to your decision. So think carefully about what these important questions are and find the appropriate opportunities to ask them in the interviewing process.

FINALIZING THE JOB OFFER

If you have done well in all the preceding steps, you are likely (although not certain) to receive an offer of employment. At this point, you can accept the offer along the terms extended by the company. Or you can try to negotiate an offer more to your liking, such as a higher salary, moving expenses (if not offered), a temporary housing allowance or arrangement until you find something suitable, or anything else you had hoped for but were not offered. The company's willingness to improve its offer will depend on company policy, how much it needs someone with your qualifications, how many other good candidates it has for the job, and how eloquently and justifiably you make your counteroffer. Of course, there is always the risk that the company will consider you ungrateful if you try to negotiate a better offer. And even if the company does agree to improve the offer, it puts greater pressure on you to perform in a superior manner once you are on the job. Nevertheless, there is usually some room for negotiation, particularly on one-time, short-term items such as relocation expenses. In addition, companies are used to expecting some kind of counteroffer from their best candidates and do not want to lose them unless their counteroffers are unreasonable.

In evaluating a job offer and, when appropriate, making a counteroffer, there are many things to consider. One thing is money. First, be careful about money illusion. Much higher living costs in some countries and cities may more than offset what appears to be a high salary. Conversely, what may appear to be a low salary may be a very good salary in locations where the cost of living is low. To assess costs of living there are several sources of information. The U.S. Department of Labor periodically publishes comparative cost-of-living indexes for major cities in the United States and, less frequently, other countries. Second, certain industries and companies within a given industry typically pay more or less money than others, regardless of location. Often, the most prestigious companies pay lower salaries because of their high prestige and the fact that they have more applicants for jobs.

Perhaps it is most important to realize there is more to a job offer than money. Other very important factors to be evaluated are the opportunities for professional development and advancement, the work environment in the company, job security, the location of the company (factors other than cost of living that are important to you), the long-term prospects for the company and its industry, the amount of travel required, and the types of people with whom you will be working. And for people seeking a career in international business, a key consideration is whether there will be opportunities to gain international experience. Any of these factors or combinations of them may make a job offer with a lower salary a better offer than it first appears if salary only is considered. In addition, if you have more than one offer to consider, these factors may make a lower salary from a less prestigious firm a better offer than a higher salary from a more prestigious company.

In considering an offer, you will also have time constraints in which to make your decision. Offers typically must be accepted or rejected within a specific number of days. If you have no other interesting viable alternatives, the decision becomes comparatively easy. However, if you have multiple offers or are expecting to receive additional offers, time constraints can become major factors in your decision. If you do not decide quickly enough, you may lose some or all of the offers you have received. This may become especially important if you have made counteroffers but have not yet received a reply or are awaiting a job offer from the company that is your first choice. As a result, you must carefully assess the probabilities of getting the job offer you want and the terms you prefer (that have not yet been offered) against the offer you have in hand with a decision deadline attached.

If all of this information about getting a job appears to be like a game, your perception is correct. It is a game in many respects. And like other games you have played and will play, you have a better chance of winning if you thoroughly understand the game, how it is played, what it takes to win, and the other players in the game.

Moving Up

Once you have a job, your performance in that job will largely influence your future advancement in the company or the possibility of getting a job with another company. If you do well, you should have many good opportunities for advancement, If it is your first job, you can usually expect to be put in some kind of orientation and training program to learn about the company, its policies, and specific ways of doing business. And in many companies, if you do not do well enough in their training program, your employment with them will end abruptly. If you enter the position with limited or no experience, during your first few years you can also usually expect to be given a lot of work and assignments that you may consider to be mundane and not terribly exciting or important. Until you can demonstrate that you have the proper skills, attitudes, and experience to do relatively simple tasks, you will not be given opportunities to do more advanced, important ones. Thus there is a kind of apprenticeship period that must first be completed satisfactorily—a period that you may find frustrating and unfulfilling. However, it is a period that is virtually inescapable, regardless of the company.

After this apprenticeship period comes your first real opportunity for advancement. However, in many cases it will still not involve international activities or responsibilities, so your patience may need to be tested again. In most companies there are formal mechanisms for announcing job openings and formal procedures for applying for openings. It is therefore important for you to become aware of and familiar with these formal mechanisms and procedures. It is also advisable to keep your ears and eyes open for potential openings, such as a pending retirement or new business opportunities being developed by the company. The company grapevine is often a good source for this kind of information, but a little homework and research on your own is also advisable. Company social activities also provide ways to meet people at higher levels and, in the process, to both learn more about advancement opportunities and make these people aware of your interests and qualifications.

Most of the international business opportunities you will have early in your career will be located in your native country. They will also typically be of a staff type rather than a managerial type. For example, you may have been working as a financial analyst in a domestic context and be given an opportunity to analyze a foreign company. Or you may have been involved in domestic purchasing and be given a project to investigate purchasing from a foreign supplier. Conversely, you may have been doing domestic market research and be given an assignment to research export opportunities. Once again, how well you do these initial tasks will influence your opportunities for being given more advanced and important ones.

Still later in your career will come opportunities for assignments abroad, at least in many companies. While foreign assignments are decreasing in percentage terms, they are still available. And they are most available for persons who have had considerable domestic experience and who also have international expertise. Not all of these opportunities will be in glamorous locations, and there are always some risks and problems involved in taking foreign assignments. If you are married, you may have problems convincing your spouse to relocate to a foreign country, particularly if you have school-age children or your spouse is also employed. There are culture shock problems to be considered and overcome in both moving abroad and in moving back to your native country once the foreign assignment is completed. There is a risk that your performance abroad will be less than what it would have been domestically due to the differences in cultural and business environments. There is a risk that whatever you do abroad will not be as noticed or appreciated as what you would have done domestically. There are also the risks and related problems of being "out of sight, out of mind" and not being as attuned to internal corporate politics.

On the other hand, a foreign assignment can be very important for future advancement in a company. It is also something you have undoubtedly hoped and prepared for that will have a lasting impact on your life both professionally and personally. It will also provide the ultimate challenge for your international abilities. Furthermore, if a foreign assignment is offered to you and you decline it, it may adversely affect your opportunities for one in the future as well as your general opportunities for advancement in the company. For all of these reasons, it is important to assess very carefully an opportunity for an assignment abroad.

Several professional matters worth investigating before you apply for or accept such an assignment are the following. Have the senior managers in the company risen to their positions by having foreign assignments? What are the company's plans for you after you have completed the foreign assignment? What skills and experiences will you gain that will be valued highly by your company or other companies for whom you might work? Are you truly prepared for all aspects of the foreign assignment? What are the career implications for you if you do not pursue the opportunity or decline the assignment? It is important to analyze answers to these questions even though they may be difficult to obtain.

Still later in your career are opportunities for advancement to senior managerial positions and potentially top management positions. An increasing number of these positions will involve global responsibilities and, as a result, require considerable experience and superior performance in domestic and international operations. In considering you for these high-level positions, firms do not just take into account what your personal accomplishments have been. They also consider how you have been able to obtain the best performance from others who have worked with and for you and the degrees of difficulty under which the work has been accomplished. An astute company will value highly international experiences and accomplishments and may, in fact, require them for promotion to top positions. However, it is a reality that some companies will not require them or value them highly. In such cases, you may have to decide whether to stay with this kind of company, move to a different one, or change careers.

Moving On

Moving on involves two different decisions: moving to a different company and moving to a different career. Each of these decisions has different costs, benefits, and risks associated with it. Probably the more difficult decision is to change your career, but both decisions involve a certain degree of uncertainty.

CHANGING COMPANIES

Moving to a different company involves deciding to stay in your current occupation but changing to a company that offers you something better professionally. Your previous experiences working for another company may be highly prized by a prospective employer. As a result, the employer may be willing to offer you faster promotion, more money, or other incentives or better benefits than those offered you by your current employer. Because of your experience, you are also in a better position to qualify for another job and to negotiate employment terms preferable to you. Becoming aware of these new opportunities and transforming them into realities involve the same basic processes as those for obtaining your initial job. However, once you have been working, you should have developed some personal and professional contacts with people in other companies, such as your firm's suppliers, customers, and, quite possibly, competitors. These contacts can be useful to you in finding out about job openings in their companies and how to apply for them.

It is not unusual for people to change companies several times during their career, especially in the Western world, because of the many advantages of doing so. The primary reasons people change companies are to get more money, to advance faster, to broaden their experience, and to gain other advantages that their current company is not providing them. It is often an unfortunate reality that another company will value your worth more than your existing company. As a result, another company will be willing to offer you more than your existing company. However, there are risks and problems in changing companies. The old cliché that the grass always looks greener on the other side of the fence often applies: the new company may not turn out to be better than your previous company. In addition, you may have problems transferring your experiences and skills to your new company. You will also have to spend considerable amounts of time and energy just learning about the operations, policies, procedures, and practices of your new company. You will also probably have to overcome the resentment of some people in your new company who think they are more qualified for the position you now occupy. If and when you try to implement changes in the way the company or those you now supervise have operated historically, you can also expect some resistance and resentment. And if you change companies too frequently, current and prospective employers may consider you to be an opportunist, unstable, disloyal, or too self-centered. Therefore, the potential advantages of changing companies must be weighed carefully against the potential disadvantages.

CHANGING CAREERS

It is quite possible that at some point you may become unhappy, bored, or in other ways dissatisfied with the career you have been pursuing. After all, you can't really know what that career and related life-style involve until you have actually experienced them. Alternatively, you may have planned from the beginning to change careers later in life or suddenly discover a new career opportunity that you consider to be better in some way than your present career. In any of these circumstances, a fundamental change in your career may occur.

In evaluating a career change, you need to consider anew all the factors you initially considered when you selected your first career. What kind of work, work pattern, and work colleagues would be involved? What kind of life-style and rewards are likely (financial, psychological, emotional, motivational, and cultural)? Do you have the proper preparation and credentials for the new career? What are the many risks involved in making the career change? What are the later options for changing back to your previous career or for moving on to still another career?

One career change that many practitioners make is to leave the world of business for academia. This type of change frequently occurs after a person has been in business for more than five years and determines that a practitioner's life is not what he or she wants. It also frequently occurs as part of a formulated plan to gain some business experience before becoming a professor of business. Finally, it frequently occurs when a practitioner is approaching retirement or has already retired. Especially in this last case, the prime motivation for the career change is to share with students the considerable real-world experiences the practitioners have accumulated during their careers in business and to add a more pragmatic dimension to students' education.

If a practitioner is considering a move to academia at the end of a long career in business, it is usually not necessary to do any additional educational preparation. Such people are typically appointed as lecturers (or adjunct faculty members) on a nontenured basis and are not usually expected to be active in research and publishing. To begin searching for such a job, it is usually sufficient to contact the dean at a college of business or the department head of the functional area that matches the practitioner's area of specialization (for example, an international marketing practitioner should contact the head of the marketing or international business department). However, not all business schools hire retired or retiring business executives, preferring to hire younger faculty with Ph.D.s and strong research and publication experience or potential. In addition, having been a successful practitioner does not guarantee that you will be a successful teacher, as many business schools and practitioners have discovered. Finally, lecturers or adjunct faculty are not paid as well as professors or anywhere near what they were paid as practitioners. But if practitioners have good retirement plans, a move to academia can provide additional income and an opportunity to enjoy an attractive life-style and to educate and influence future business leaders.

On the other hand, if the career change to academia comes early in a practitioner's life and is expected to be reasonably permanent, obtaining a doctoral degree is a virtual necessity. Very few business schools will accept anything less. In addition, a faculty member will need the further education and the research and teaching skills provided by a doctoral program in order to get promoted and tenured once he or she is teaching at a university. Some exceptions can be found at smaller colleges, community colleges, branch campuses of larger colleges, and technical education institutions. However, if it is in the prestigious colleges and universities you seek employment, do not rely too heavily on that exception. Instead, be prepared to go back to school and comparative poverty for three to five years in order to obtain a doctoral degree.

Another possible and frequently pursued career change for a practitioner who has been working in a large company is to enter the exciting world of entrepreneurship—become self-employed. For example, people who have been working in international marketing for multinational firms often start their own export marketing or management company. In other cases, people who have been working abroad for many years start their own consulting companies to advise other companies how to do business abroad. Or people who have been involved in marketing research or political risk research in a large company start their own research company.

While there is more risk (less job security) in entrepreneurship than in working for a large company, there are offsetting advantages, such as being in charge instead of having to work for someone else. At the same time, however, you will need some capital to get started and sufficient experience to make the venture a success. It is also possible to make a career change in the opposite direction, from being an entrepreneur to becoming an employee of a larger company.

Another career change is to enter politics or other types of government service. The administrative abilities and international experiences of a successful international business practitioner can be valuable qualifications for many types of government careers. Examples include elected positions and positions in foreign service or the departments of commerce, science and technology, labor, agriculture, and transportation. These positions can be at the local, state, or national level. Taking such a position need not be a permanent career change. Many times, successful practitioners take a temporary leave of absence for a government job and then return to their practitioner careers. A main attraction to making a career change to government service is the opportunity to influence public policy decisions. Another is to try to make government more efficient.

In sum, making a major career change will involve the kinds of uncertainties and risks that are involved in choosing your initial career. However, you will know a great deal more about one career (the one you are in) and will be presumably older, wiser, and more certain of your likes and dislikes. All of these factors should help you make wiser decisions about career alternatives and how to make a successful career change if that is what you decide to do.

ACADEMIC CAREERS

Getting Your Initial Job

The basic process of getting an academic job is similar in most respects to getting a practitioner job. You must learn where positions are available, how to apply for them, and how ultimately to obtain the position you want on the terms you want.

BECOMING AWARE OF JOB OPPORTUNITIES

There are fewer publications that carry advertisements for academic positions. General print media such as newspapers and magazines seldom carry advertisements for academic positions other than administrative, such as department chairpersons, deans, vice-presidents, and presidents. One notable exception is the *Chronicle of Higher Education,* which carries advertisements for all types of academic positions. Other printed sources of information about positions available are academic journals and newsletters of academic associations. The Academy of International Business, the Academy of Management, the American Accounting Association, the American Marketing Association, and the Financial Management Association are examples of associations with newsletters. To access these newsletters, you must usually become a member of the organization or know someone who receives the newsletter. Other job leads can be obtained from notices posted on bulletin boards in most universities or from directly contacting faculty or administrators. Even if there are no positions suitable for you at your contacts' universities, they may know of a position at another university that might be suitable for you. And if you are still in a degree program, the faculty at your university are an excellent source of job leads and contacts. In fact, they are probably your best source of leads, contacts, and other information pertinent to your job search. Finally, and perhaps most uniquely to academia, there are job placement activities and services at the annual meetings of major academic associations. However, attending these meetings and being able to make use of any job placement service they provide normally requires that you become a member.

Descriptions of positions available typically specify the functional specialization sought, the level of the position, the duties to be performed, the qualifications necessary or preferred, and other major preferences and expectations. In examining this information, look for specific references to international duties and qualifications and whether they are necessary, important, or desired. Position descriptions also typically contain information about the institution's history, size, degree programs, and other factors that might entice you to apply.

Additional information about specific universities can be found in libraries and academic counseling centers.

Once you have identified potentially suitable positions, the next step is to send a letter expressing your interest and suitability for the position available. Or, if you do not know for certain that a position is available, send a letter expressing your interest in the kind of position you are seeking. A professional resume should always be enclosed, explaining in great detail your research and teaching interests, your academic and other qualifications, honors you have received, articles you have had published, and any other information pertinent to the position sought. Unlike the resume for a practitioner job, the resume for an academic job should not be brief. In general, length is better than brevity.

The recruiting period for most academic jobs begins in late summer the year before the position is actually available. The reason is two-fold. Most academic jobs are on an academic-year basis that begins in late August or early September, and most major academic associations hold their annual meetings in late summer or during the fall. Because the annual meetings are often the first face-to-face contact between candidates and employers, a considerable period of time is necessary to complete the hiring process, hence the almost one-year lag between the time the recruiting process starts and the job actually begins. You should contact potential employers before the annual meetings of the academic associations, and you should attend the most appropriate meetings. Most universities send faculty to these meetings and also conduct preliminary interviews. Therefore, in order to get interviews scheduled at these meetings, you need to make contact ahead of time. Even if you have not been able to arrange an interview beforehand, you may be able to arrange a short interview while at the meeting. But it is a higher risk strategy. You should also make use of any job placement service at the meetings. In most cases, there are means of making your resume available to others attending the meeting who may also be recruiting for their universities. The placement service also usually provides announcements of positions available about which you may have been unaware. Faculty members from your university who are attending the meeting can be of great assistance in introducing you to faculty from potential universities who are also attending the meeting.

INTERVIEWING

Without getting a preliminary interview at one of the meetings of an academic association, it will be very difficult to get invited to an interview at the campus of a university. And without an interview on campus it is virtually impossible for you to get a job offer. Furthermore, you will not have an opportunity to see the campus, the community in which it is located, or meet the rest of the faculty and important administrators unless you are willing to do so at your own expense. For all of these reasons, interviews you have at association meetings are vitally important.

The general advice given earlier in this chapter concerning interview preparation and techniques for practitioner jobs applies equally to academic job interviews. In other words, be thoroughly prepared to both look sharp and be sharp. While it is true that some academics are eccentric and, in general, place less emphasis on clothes and general appearance than practitioners do, it is still advisable to look your best. And business school faculty generally dress more formally than faculty in other departments of the university.

During your preliminary interview, you will be expected to provide information about your specific research and teaching interests and the content of your dissertation (or the progress you are making on your dissertation if you have not completed it). The faculty interviewing you may also test your knowledge of specific subject matter pertinent to your field of specialization. The interviewer will also be looking for indications of your compatibility with existing members of the faculty, including personality traits, research abilities and interests, teaching abilities and interests, and professional goals and attitudes. The more preparation you have done before the interview, the better you will be able to demonstrate these kinds of compatibilities and, in general, the better impression you will make during the interview.

If you are given an opportunity to be interviewed on campus, be prepared to experience several days of the same kinds of interviews with faculty members who have not yet met you and even with those you have already met. In addition, be prepared to give a formal presentation about your dissertation to a group of faculty and possibly a guest lecture to a class of students. You can also expect to be interviewed by a senior administrator of the school of business and possibly the university. It is also likely that you will have some kind of social activity while on campus and be given an opportunity to see the community.

By virtue of the fact that you have been invited to the campus for an interview, you are well down the road to receiving an offer. As your visit to the university is likely to be the only one you will have before making a decision, you need to make the most of your visit. Therefore, you should ask to see and learn about the things at the university and in the community that are most important to your decision. Examples include library and computer facilities, offices, secretarial and related support services, research support, teaching loads, promotion and tenure criteria and related processes, housing, cultural amenities, and, of course, financial information such as salary, benefits, and retirement packages.

FINALIZING A JOB OFFER

Following an on-campus interview, you can expect to wait anywhere from several weeks to several months before you learn whether an offer will be forthcoming. The two factors that most influence the length of this waiting period are how early in the recruiting cycle you had your on-campus interview and how highly you rank on the university's list of candidates. If you were one of the first to be interviewed, you will probably have a longer waiting period because the university will want to finish interviewing all leading candidates. If you do not rank as highly on the list of candidates, your waiting period is also likely to be longer because the university will first offer the position to someone ranked higher.

When you do receive an offer, you can try to negotiate more favorable terms, such as a higher salary; a lower teaching load; summer research support; a personal computer; relocation expenses; or the all-important, close-in parking spot. Your ability to achieve a better offer will depend on your negotiating ability, how much the university wants you, and what flexibility it has in making the final offer. It is generally true that less prestigious universities have a greater predisposition to negotiate. And most universities will do more negotiating on one-time expenditures than they will on longer-term expenditures. They will also be more willing and able to negotiate if you have completed your dissertation.

Other alternatives to getting an initial job in academia are to seek a lecturer, adjunct, or visiting position or to seek an administrative position. All of these positions are considered nontenure track in the sense that the possibilities for obtaining tenure do not exist. These positions are typically on a year-to-year contract, and many do not require a doctoral degree. Nontenure positions are typically offered when it is not possible for a tenure-track position to be offered or filled.

Advancing in Your Career

In all but a few rare cases, initial tenure-track jobs in academia are at the assistant professor level. At most universities, promotion to the next level (associate professor) requires a minimum of five years of continuous service and the meeting or surpassing of specified promotion criteria. For promotion to full professor, a similar time period and evaluation process exists. Therefore, it is rare that someone move in the ranks from being an assistant professor to a full professor in fewer than ten years. A more typical time period is twelve to thirteen years. However, there is no guarantee of promotion, and some faculty remain at lower levels throughout their career.

Typical criteria considered for promotion are research and publications, teaching performance, and service activities. In the research/publication area, more specific factors evaluated are the number of publications, the types of journals in which they are published, and their contributions to knowledge. In the teaching area, factors considered are the number and level of courses taught and various measures of teaching performance, such as student and peer evaluations. In the service area, service to the university, the profession, and the community are generally considered and evaluated, although generally speaking, service to the university and the profession count more heavily.

To be promoted to associate professor, most universities expect superior performance in at least one of these three areas (research, teaching, service) and no less than average performance in the other two. To be promoted to full professor, most universities require superior performance in at least two of the areas and average or above average performance in the remaining area.

These same factors are also considered and evaluated in tenure decisions. The awarding of tenure is a major milestone in an academic's career. While it is not an absolute guarantee of lifetime employment, it is the nearest thing to it. The practice of tenure was established to guarantee academic freedom in universities and in essence means that a faculty member cannot be fired for expressing controversial opinions or teaching controversial subject matter. While this is still an important aspect of tenure today, it has also come to mean that a faculty member has a reasonable expectation of being employed each subsequent year. Until you are granted tenure, your employment contract is on a year-to-year basis. In most circumstances, you must be granted tenure during or before your seventh year of employment or your employment at the university will be terminated.

At most universities, the tenure and promotion process are separate. In other words, promotion does not automatically result in tenure, or tenure in promotion. This is also true for salary increases. It is normal practice to receive salary increases without being promoted or granted tenure. And while tenure does not affect salary, promotion typically brings with it a salary increase. Salary increases are generally based on the same criteria as those for promotion and tenure but are also influenced by the total amount of money available for allocation and the university's desire to keep you. In sum, salary increases, promotion, and tenure are all based on largely the same performance criteria. Those who do a better job of publishing, teaching, and providing service will advance faster in all areas than those who do not.

For academics specializing in international business, advancement can be more complicated and difficult if they are not in an international business department. In most universities, there is not an international business department. As a result, most international business faculty members are housed in a functional area department such as management, accounting, finance, or marketing. In most cases, they are expected to teach classes, conduct research, and publish in these functional areas on both international and noninternational subjects. They are also evaluated on criteria used to evaluate noninternationally oriented faculty. If international business faculty members spend all of their time doing only internationally oriented research and teaching, they may have more difficulty getting promoted and tenured in a functional area department. Therefore, promotion and tenure realities may require an appropriate division of effort between international and noninternational activities in teaching, research, and service. This is why it is so important for academics specializing in international business to investigate thoroughly the promotion and tenure process and criteria at each specific university before accepting a job.

Moving On

In academia, you may subsequently find it desirable to change employers or your career for the same reasons that a practitioner may choose to do so. Changing employers within academia involves some change and risk but less than changing your career.

Starting at a new university entails having to learn a whole new set of university policies and procedures and how the new university's system works. Until you have learned the new system and how to make it work for you, you will probably experience some confusion, frustration, and loss of productivity. In addition, at the new university many fewer people know who you are and what your interests and capabilities are. So you will have to begin all over again proving yourself and making yourself known. A move to a new university also normally requires a move to a new city because only the largest metropolitan areas have multiple universities from which to select. In addition, you may not be able to transfer from a tenured position at your current university to a tenured position at your new university or may not be given full credit at your new university for all your years of service at your current university. Finally, there is always the risk that you will not like the new university as much as you expected and perhaps less than your previous university.

Despite these problems and risks, changing universities can result in faster promotion, bigger increases in salary, better colleagues with whom to work, more interesting teaching and research opportunities, and a host of new experiences. Like getting your initial job, however, there must be a suitable match between you and the position at the new university. The basic procedure for getting a subsequent job is the same as for getting your initial job. The main advantage you have in getting a subsequent job is your experience—provided that you have a good track record.

Assuming you began your academic career as a faculty member, another type of career change within academia is to become an administrator. The normal ladder of progression is to become chairman of an academic department, then an assistant dean, associate dean, and dean, then move up into the university administration: vice-president, senior vice-president, and president. Of course, there are always exceptions to this pattern of progression, particularly if you move to smaller universities or if you have some special talents in high demand by your current or prospective university. For example, as an international specialist, you may become an assistant or associate dean without having been a department chair because your university did not have an international business department. Or because a college of business decides it needs a dean with international expertise to increase its international activities, you might become a dean without having been an assistant or associate dean if you have significant international expertise and some administrative experience.

Regardless of the precise progression, a move to administration involves some fundamental changes in your work activities and responsibilities. You will do less teaching and research, will probably shift from a nine-month contract to a twelve-month contract (reducing your summer options), have less contact with students, and much more paperwork. You will also have more meetings to conduct and attend, budgets to deal with, more regular work hours, and many more administrative headaches. On the other hand, administration offers new challenges and opportunities without having to leave the university environment. In addition, the move does not have to be permanent. Many administrators return to faculty positions after having been administrators for a period of time.

More drastic forms of moving on are to leave academia for government service or to become a business practitioner. Your experience as a researcher or administrator can serve as a springboard to either of these alternative careers. Many academics find employment in government agencies where their knowledge and research skills are needed. For example, international business faculty can find employment in international divisions of departments of commerce at the state or federal level and also in departments of state, labor, education, agriculture, transportation, or tourism. Some academics also enter the corporate world or go into business for themselves by starting their own manufacturing or consulting firm.

Leaving academia does involve a significant change in life-style, generally to one that is more hectic, high pressured and possibly less secure. However, the change is often to a higher paying career and one that you may find offers you other benefits that academia is not providing you. Furthermore, a move out of academia does not have to be permanent, nor does it have to be total. Being in business or government service for a period of time can make you a better academic and also increase your attractiveness to universities. Some universities will permit you to take a leave of absence to gain these nonacademic experiences, particularly if the university believes that you and it will benefit ultimately. In addition, most universities permit some time for faculty to do consulting or other forms of practitioner activities while still employed at the university. The key criterion is that these external activities do not interfere with your academic performance and responsibilities.

In academia and business, your initial career choice is not an irrevocable one. You can change within academia, move out and back into academia, and, to some degree, have an academic and nonacademic career simultaneously. If you start in a business career, you can change within business, shift out of and into business, and, in some cases, do some nonbusiness activities while you are still a practitioner.

As a general rule, the more your specific knowledge and skills are valued, the more possible it will be to make changes or to do several things concurrently. Also, the more your skills are transferable from one career to another, the greater the possibilities are for changing careers successfully. Finally, how well you do in whatever career you are in will influence how quickly you progress in that career and also how attractive you appear to a different employer (in the same career or a new career).

As should be evident by now, there are many excellent opportunities for international business specialists in business, academia, and government service. In addition, these opportunities are increasing throughout the world in number, variety, and importance. While each career has its unique advantages and disadvantages, they are not mutually exclusive. Moreover, due to their international dimension, international business careers all offer significant intellectual, psychological, emotional, and cultural challenges. Like any career, they are not without their risks and frustrations. But if the past is predictive of the future, international business will continue to increase in importance and with it the demand for international business experts. Therefore, regardless of the type of career in international business you select and regardless of whether you remain in that initial career, a specialization in international business will offer you many significant challenges, rewards, and employment opportunities. And based on the experiences of those who have chosen international business as their specialization, it also offers an enriching and satisfying life-style.

A Complete list of titles in our extensive *Opportunities In* series

OPPORTUNITIES IN

Accounting
Acting
Advertising
Aerospace
Agriculture
Airline
Animal & Pet Care
Architecture
Automotive Service
Banking
Beauty Culture
Biological Sciences
Biotechnology
Book Publishing
Broadcasting
Building Construction
  Trades
Business Communication
Business Management
Cable Television
CAD/CAM
Carpentry
Chemistry
Child Care
Chiropractic
Civil Engineering
Cleaning Service
Commercial Art & Graphic
  Design
Computer Maintenance
Computer Science
Counseling & Development
Crafts
Culinary
Customer Service
Data Processing
Dental Care
Desktop Publishing
Direct Marketing
Drafting
Electrical Trades
Electronics
Energy
Engineering
Engineering Technology
Environmental
Eye Care
Fashion
Fast Food
Federal Government

Film
Financial
Fire Protection Services
Fitness
Food Services
Foreign Language
Forestry
Health & Medical
High Tech
Home Economics
Homecare Services
Horticulture
Hospital Administration
Hotel & Motel Management
Human Resource
  Management
Information Systems
Installation & Repair
Insurance
Interior Design
International Business
Journalism
Laser Technology
Law
Law Enforcement &
  Criminal Justice
Library & Information
  Science
Machine Trades
Magazine Publishing
Marine & Maritime
Marketing
Masonry
Medical Imaging
Medical Technology
Metalworking
Military
Modeling
Music
Newspaper Publishing
Nonprofit Organizations
Nursing
Nutrition
Occupational Therapy
Office Occupations
Paralegal
Paramedical
Part-time & Summer Jobs
Performing Arts
Petroleum
Pharmacy

Photography
Physical Therapy
Physician
Physician Assistant
Plastics
Plumbing & Pipe Fitting
Postal Service
Printing
Property Management
Psychology
Public Health
Public Relations
Purchasing
Real Estate
Recreation & Leisure
Refrigeration & Air
  Conditioning
Religious Service
Restaurant
Retailing
Robotics
Sales
Secretarial
Social Science
Social Work
Speech-Language Patholog
Sports & Athletics
Sports Medicine
State & Local Government
Teaching
Technical Writing &
  Communications
Telecommunications
Telemarketing
Television & Video
Theatrical Design &
  Production
Tool & Die
Transportation
Travel
Trucking
Veterinary Medicine
Visual Arts
Vocational & Technical
Warehousing
Waste Management
Welding
Word Processing
Writing
Your Own Service Business

VGM Career Horizons
a division of *NTC Publishing Group*
4255 West Touhy Avenue
Lincolnwood, Illinois 60646–1975